JONES & BARTLETT LEARNING INFORMATION SYSTEMS SECURITY & ASSURANCE SERIES

LABORATORY MANUAL TO ACCOMPANY

Fundamentals of Information Systems Security

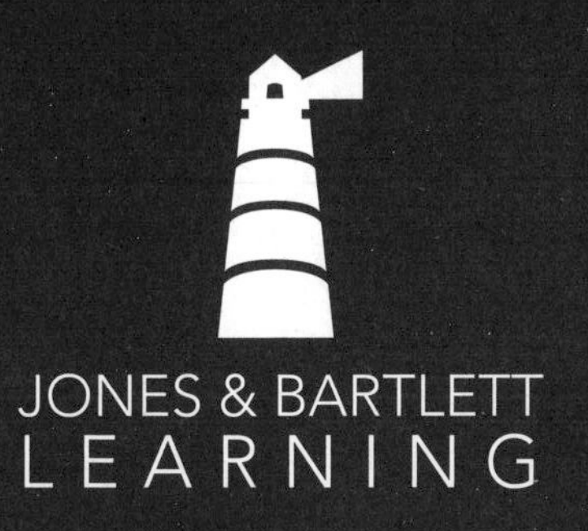

World Headquarters
Jones & Bartlett Learning
40 Tall Pine Drive
Sudbury, MA 01776
978-443-5000
info@jblearning.com
www.jblearning.com

Jones & Bartlett Learning Canada
6339 Ormindale Way
Mississauga, Ontario L5V 1J2
Canada

Jones & Bartlett Learning International
Barb House, Barb Mews
London W6 7PA
United Kingdom

Jones & Bartlett Learning books and products are available through most bookstores and online booksellers. To contact Jones & Bartlett Learning directly, call 800-832-0034, fax 978-443-8000, or visit our website, www.jblearning.com.

Substantial discounts on bulk quantities of Jones & Bartlett Learning publications are available to corporations, professional associations, and other qualified organizations. For details and specific discount information, contact the special sales department at Jones & Bartlett Learning via the above contact information or send an email to specialsales@jblearning.com.

Production Credits
Chief Executive Officer: Ty Field
President: James Homer
SVP, Chief Operating Officer: Don Jones, Jr.
SVP, Chief Technology Officer: Dean Fossella
SVP, Chief Marketing Officer: Alison M. Pendergast
SVP, Chief Financial Officer: Ruth Siporin
SVP, Curriculum Solutions: Christopher Will
VP, Design and Production: Anne Spencer
VP, Manufacturing and Inventory Control: Therese Connell
Author: vLab Solutions, LLC, David Kim, President
Editorial Management: Perspectives, Inc., Phil Graham, President
Reprints and Special Projects Manager: Susan Schultz
Associate Production Editor: Tina Chen
Director of Marketing: Alisha Weisman
Associate Marketing Manager: Meagan Norlund
Cover Design: Anne Spencer
Composition: vLab Solutions, LLC
Cover Image: © ErickN/ShutterStock, Inc.
Printing and Binding: Malloy, Inc.
Cover Printing: Malloy, Inc.

ISBN: 978-1-4496-1214-6

6048
Printed in the United States of America
14 13 12 10 9 8 7 6 5 4

Table of Contents

ISS Curriculum Overview

The Bachelor of Science degree in Information Systems Security (ISS) is comprised of twelve foundational courses, each of which has 10 labs. The students will perform paper-based labs (design, configuration, or analysis) and hands-on labs using real equipment, security tools, and applications.

The ISS curriculum is comprised of the following courses:

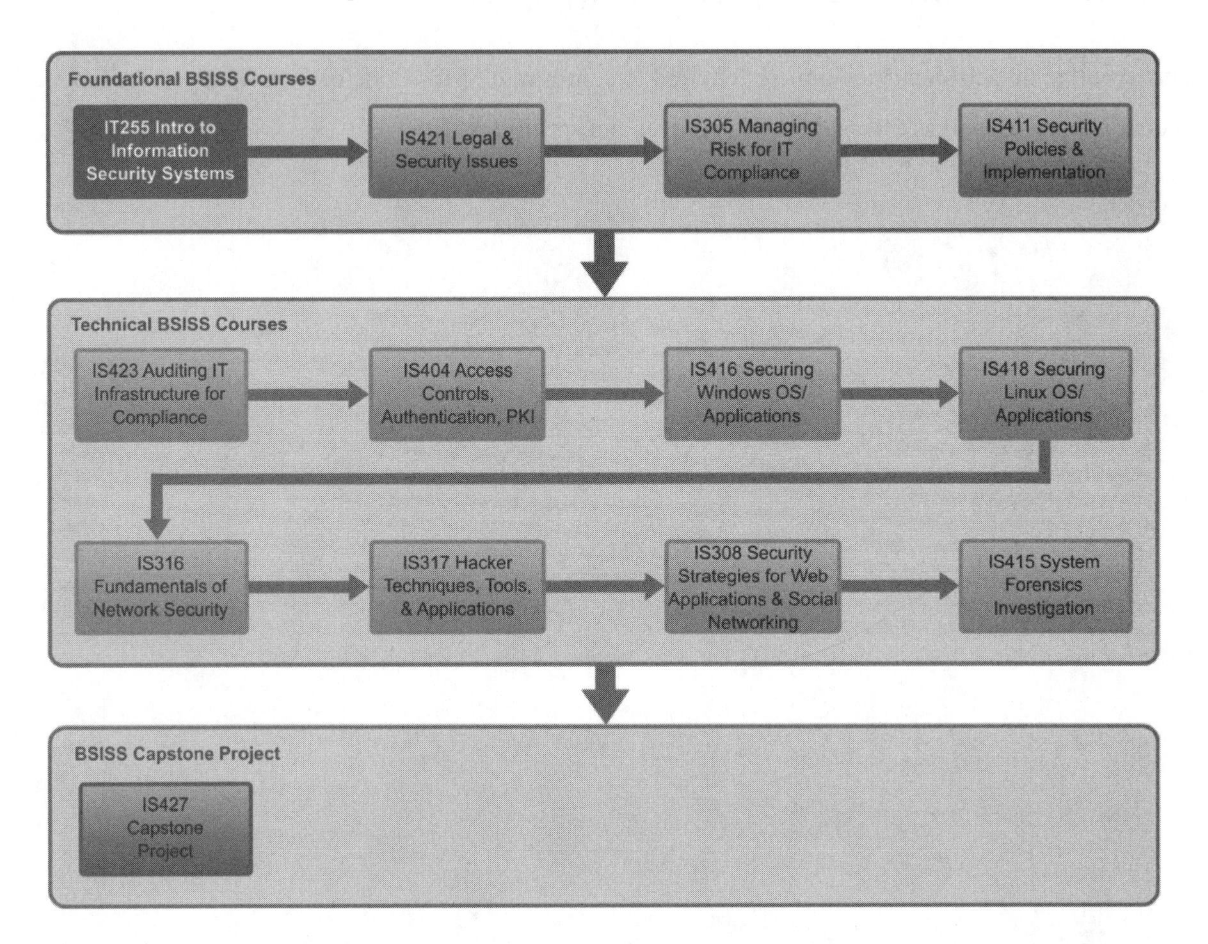

The introductory level courses, identified in red above, have paper-based labs with some accompanying hands-on labs. The security practitioner courses, in green above, have substantial, hands-on lab exercises requiring students to be proficient with hardware, software, tools, and applications commonly found within the seven domains of a typical IT infrastructure. The IS427 Capstone Project course is the final course that the ISS student takes prior to graduating from the program. This course encompasses all the accumulated knowledge obtained from the entire ISS curriculum and requires the student to respond to an RFP for information systems security consulting.

Ethics and Code of Conduct

Students enrolled in the ISS curriculum are aware that the hardware, software, tools, and applications presented and used within the ISS curriculum are for instructional and educational purposes only.

The students are not to use these tools, applications, or techniques on live production IT infrastructures. Under no circumstances shall they use the tools, applications, or techniques on ITT Technical Institute or the production IT infrastructures and networks of other organizations.

Students enrolled in the ISS curriculum are required to conform to ITT's Code of Conduct described in the student manual as well as the institution's general and specific policies.

Laboratory #1 ISS 316 Security #1

Lab #1: Perform Reconnaissance & Probing Using ZenMap GUI (Nmap)

Learning Objectives and Outcomes

Upon completing this lab, students will be able to perform the following tasks:

- Obtain, access, and copy the Virtual Machines (server farm and workstations) needed for IT255 onto your removable hard drive
- Use VMware Player to enable and power-up the VMs (server farm and workstations) needed for this hands-on lab
- Plan an initial reconnaissance and probing attack on the ISS "Mock" IT Infrastructure
- Use ZenMap GUI (Nmap) to perform an "Intense Scan" on the entire targeted ISS "Mock" IT Infrastructure 172.30.0.0/24
- Generate a ZenMap GUI (Nmap) port scanning report and submit as part of your hands-on lab deliverables

Required Setup and Tools

This lab requires the use of the ITT "Mock" IT Infrastructure and Virtualized Server Farm.

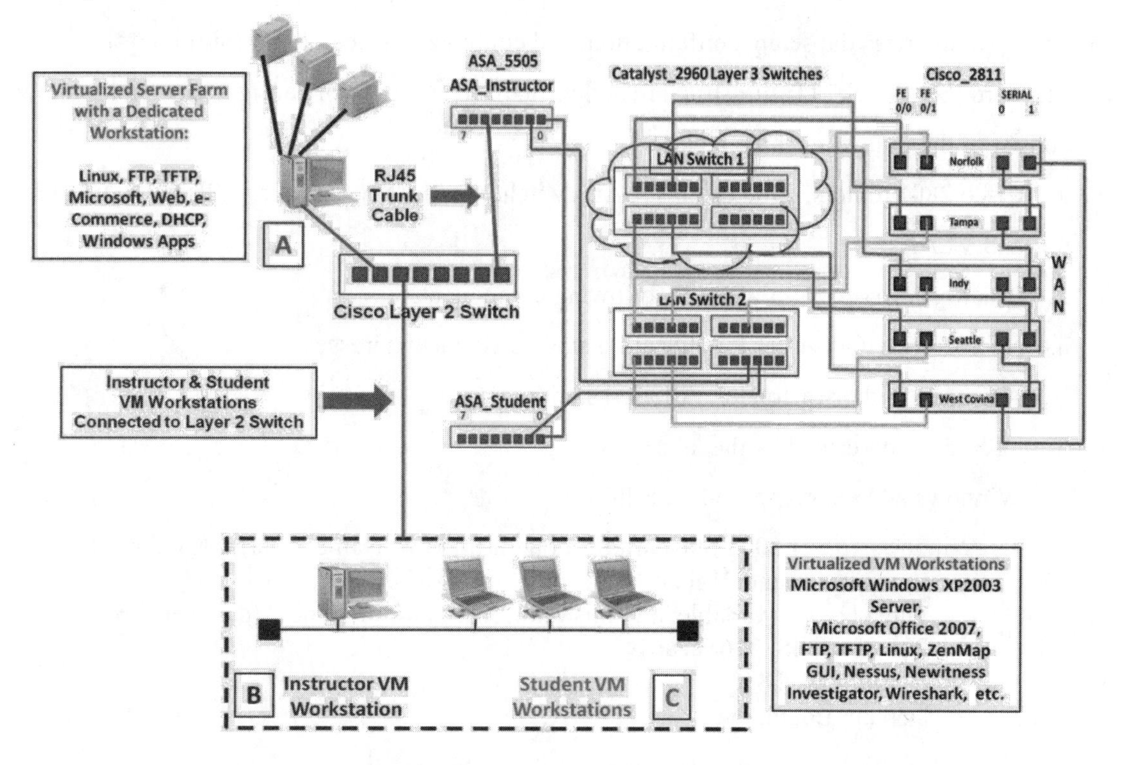

Figure 1 – ISS Onsite "Mock" IT Infrastructure & Virtualized Server Farm

The "Mock" IT Infrastructure is a preconfigured IP network infrastructure complete with a classroom Cisco WAN and a virtualized server farm. All IP-addressing schema, VLAN configurations, and layer 2/3 switching is pre-configured. The IP networking infrastructure remains static and only needs the following removable parts:

A) A classroom workstation (with at least 2 Gig RAM/4 Gig RAM recommended) capable of supporting a removable hard drive containing the virtualized server farm. This classroom workstation will support the virtualized server farm and connects to the same layer 2 switch as the Instructor and Student VM workstations. This layer 2 switch is then connected to ASA_Instructor for entry into the IP networking infrastructure via an RJ45 trunk cable (refer to Figure 1) using 172.30.0.1 255.255.255.0 as the IP default gateway router

B) An instructor workstation (with at least 2 Gig RAM) that shall act as the instructor's demo VM workstation. He/she will display the Instructor VM workstation on the LCD projector to demonstrate enabling and powering the VM server farm and VM workstation and for performing the hands-on lab

C) The student' classroom workstations isolated on a layer 2 switch for connectivity to the ISS "Mock" IT Infrastructure via a trunk cable to ASA_Instructor. These workstations will support the Student VM workstation and Target VM servers locally

The following summarizes the setup, configuration, and equipment needed to perform Lab #1:

1. Standard ISS "Mock" IT infrastructure and virtualized server farm configuration and setup which consist of the following components:
   a. Cisco 2801 routers, 2960 catalyst LAN switches, and ASA 5505 firewalls with OSPF core and VLANs
2. A Virtualized Server Farm with the following components:
   a. Microsoft DHCP server for allocating student IP host addresses
   b. A Student and/or Instructor VM workstation
3. Target VMs as described by the lab:
   a. Windows 2003 Server Standard Edition
      - Windows Server 2003 Standard Edition 32-bit (VM Name: "TargetWindows01")
        - Computer Name: Windows02
        - Three Users Available: administrator, instructor or student (case sensitive)
        - Password: ISS316Security
        - IP Address: DHCP
        - Domain Login: NO
      - FTP (Filezilla FTP Server)

    - Port: 21
    - Username: instructor or student
    - Password: <blank>

  - TFTP (Tftpd32 TFTP Server)
    - Port: 69
    - Username: <none>
    - Password: <blank>

b. Ubuntu Desktop 9.10 Linux

  - Ubuntu Linux 9.10 Desktop Edition (VM Name: "TargetUbuntu02")
    - Computer Name: Ubuntu02
    - Two Users Available: instructor or student <case sensitive>
    - Password: ISS316Security (case sensitive)
    - IP Address: DHCP

c. Ubuntu Server 10.04 Linux Target

  - Ubuntu Linux 10.04 LTS Server (VM Name: "TargetUbuntu01")
    - Computer Name: Ubuntu01
    - **ONE** User available ONLY: administrator <case sensitive>
    - Password: ISS316Security (case sensitive)
    - IP Address: eth0 set to DHCP, eth1 and eth2 not set.

  - SSH
    - Port: 21
    - Username: administrator <case sensitive>
    - Password: <blank>

  - Apache running "Damn Vulnerable Web App" (DVWA)
    - URL: http://<serveripaddress>/dvwa
    - Password: password
    - Username: admin

4. Security and CLI tools
5. Standard ITT onsite student workstation must have the following software applications loaded to perform this lab:
   a. VMware Player 3.x
   b. Microsoft Office 2007 or higher for Lab Assessment Questions & Answers

Hands-on Lab #1 – Student Steps:

This lab will introduce the students to applications and tools commonly used by hackers and information systems security practitioners. Ethical hacking, penetration testing, and security assessments will be discussed as they learn how to perform reconnaissance and probing tasks. For this lab, the students will perform the following steps:

1. Connect the student removable hard drive to your workstation
2. Boot up the "Student" VM, and obtain an IP address from the "DHCPWindows01" VM server connected to the same layer 2 switch as your student VM workstation
3. Enable your DOS command prompt and type "ipconfig" and "ping" your allocated IP host address 172.30.0.__ , the DHCP server 172.30.0.10, and the IP default gateway router 172.30.0.1

> **NOTE:** If the workstations in your physical classroom have only 2GB of RAM then only two VMs can be powered-on at once. You only need to power-on your Student VM workstation since the DHCP server is part of the VM server farm.

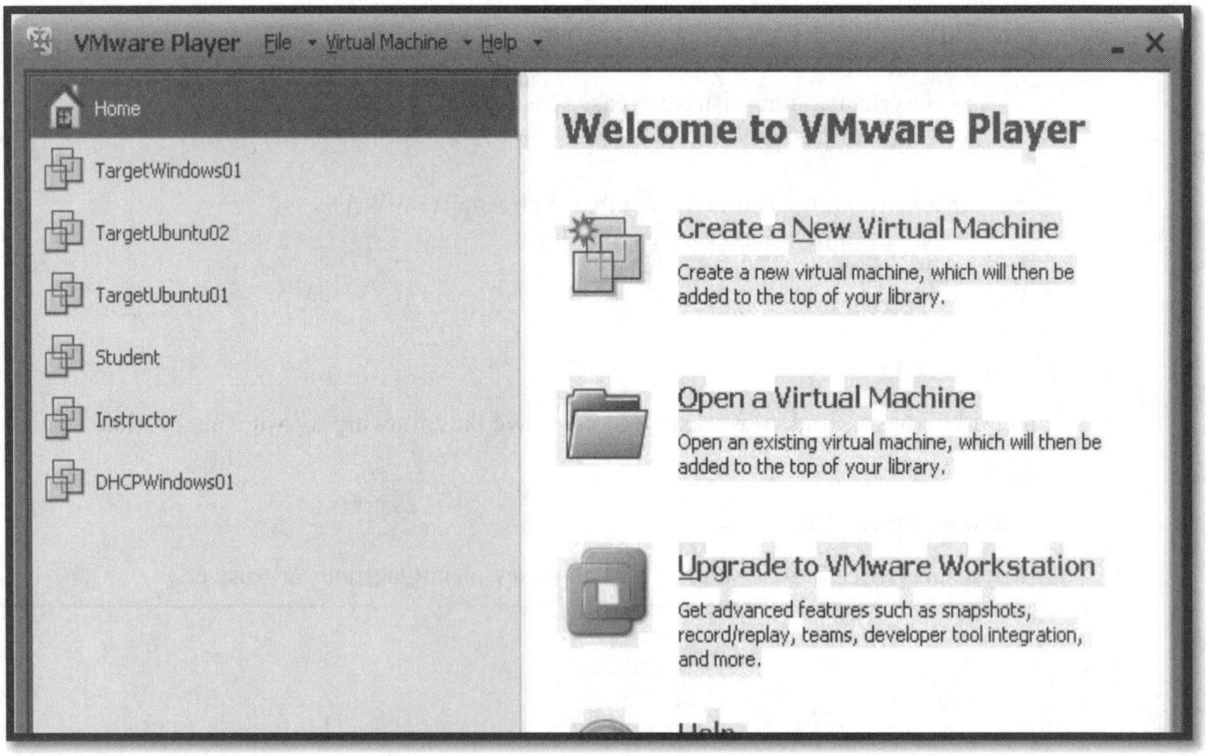

Figure 2 – VMware Player with Virtualized Server Farm

4. The Student VM workstation has the following pre-loaded applications and tools which will be used throughout this course and other ISS curriculum courses:
   a. PuTTY – for Telnet and SSH
   b. Filezilla – for FTP
   c. tftpd32 – for TFTP
   d. Wireshark – for packet capture and protocol analysis
   e. Netwitness Investigator – for packet importing and protocol analysis
   f. Nessus® - for vulnerability assessment scanning
   g. ZenMap GUI – for IP discovery, port and services scanning
5. Enable your DOS command prompt and type "ipconfig" and "ping" your allocated IP host address 172.30.0.__ , the DHCP server 172.30.0.10, and the IP default gateway router 172.30.0.1
6. Run the PuTTY application from the Instructor VM and TELNET or SSH to the ASA_Instructor (172.30.0.1), LAN.SW1 (172.16.8.5), LAN.SW2 (172.20.8.5), WestCovina (172.20.8.1), and Norfolk (172.16.8.1) routers
7. When you connect to a Cisco switch or router, enter the user name of "cisco" and terminal console password of "cisco." Then type "show ip route" and "show run" to display the Cisco core backbone network's configuration
8. From the Student VM desktop, enable ZenMap GUI, and load the Nmap application
9. Perform a "Ping Scan" or "Quick Scan" on 172.30.0.0/24 to identify all the hosts on the local subnetwork
10. Perform an "Intense Scan" on 172.30.0.0/24, and capture the results in the Nmap report
11. Save the results of your "Intense Scan," and submit them as part of your lab deliverables

Deliverables

Upon completion of this lab, the students are required to submit the following deliverables as part of this lab:

1. Lab #1 – Softcopy of the ZenMap GUI "Intense Scan" report performed
2. Lab #1 – Assessment Questions & Answers

Evaluation Criteria and Rubrics

The following are the evaluation criteria and rubrics for Lab #1 that the students must perform:

1. Was the student able to obtain, access and copy the Virtual Machines (server farm and workstations) needed for IT255 onto your removable hard drive? – [**20%**]
2. Was the student able to use VMware Player to enable and power-up the VMs (server farm and workstations) needed for this hands-on lab? – [**20%**]
3. Was the student able to plan an initial reconnaissance and probing attack on the ISS "Mock" IT Infrastructure? – [**20%**]
4. Was the student able to use ZenMap GUI (Nmap) to perform an "Intense Scan" on the entire targeted ISS "Mock" IT Infrastructure 172.30.0.0/24? – [**20%**]
5. Was the student able to generate a ZenMap GUI (Nmap) port scanning report and submit as part of your hands-on lab deliverables? – [**20%**]

Lab #1 – Assessment Worksheet

Perform Reconnaissance & Probing Using ZenMap GUI (Nmap)

Course Name & Number: ______________________________

Student Name: ______________________________

Instructor Name: ______________________________

Lab Due Date: ______________________________

Overview

Hackers traditionally follow a 5-step approach to seek out and destroy targeted hosts. The first step in performing an attack is to plan the attack by identifying your target and learning as much as possible about the target. Hackers traditionally perform an initial reconnaissance & probing scan to identify IP hosts, open ports, and services enabled on servers and workstations. In this lab, students will plan an attack on 172.30.0.0/24 where the VM server farm resides. Using ZenMap GUI, students will then perform a "Ping Scan" or "Quick Scan" on the targeted IP subnetwork.

Lab Assessment Questions & Answers

1. Name at least five applications and tools pre-loaded on the Windows 2003 Server Target VM (VM Name: "WindowsTarget01") and identify whether that application starts as a service on the system or must be run manually?

2. What was the DHCP allocated source IP host address for the Student VM, DHCP Server, and IP default gateway router?

3. Did the targeted IP hosts respond to the ICMP echo-request packet with an ICMP echo-reply packet when you initiated the "ping" command at your DOS prompt? If yes, how many ICMP echo-request packets were sent back to the IP source?

4. If you ping the "WindowsTarget01" VM server and the "UbuntuTarget01" VM server, which fields in the ICMP echo-request / echo-replies vary?

5. What is the command line syntax for running an "Intense Scan" with ZenMap on a target subnet of 172.30.0.0/24?

6. Name at least 5 different scans that may be performed from the ZenMap GUI and document under what circumstances you would choose to run those particular scans.

7. How many different tests (i.e., scripts) did your "Intense Scan" definition perform? List them all after reviewing the scan report.

8. Describe what each of these tests or scripts performs within the ZenMap GUI (Nmap) scan report.

9. How many total IP hosts (not counting Cisco device interfaces) did ZenMap GUI (Nmap) find on the network?

10. Based on your Nmap scan results and initial reconnaissance & probing, what next steps would you perform on the VM server farm and VM workstation targets?

Current Version Date: 12/06/2010

Laboratory #2

Lab #2: Perform a Vulnerability Assessment Scan Using Nessus®

(Nessus® is a Registered Trademark of Tenable Network Security, Inc.)

Learning Objectives and Outcomes

Upon completing this lab, students will be able to complete the following tasks:

- Identify risks, threats, and vulnerabilities in an IP network infrastructure using ZenMap GUI (Nmap) to perform an IP host, port, and services scan
- Perform a vulnerability assessment scan on a targeted IP subnetwork using Nessus®
- Compare the results of the ZenMap GUI "Intense Scan" with a Nessus® vulnerability assessment scan
- Assess the findings of the vulnerability assessment scan and identify critical vulnerabilities
- Make recommendations for mitigating the identified risks, threats, and vulnerabilities as described on the CVE database listing

Required Setup and Tools

This lab requires the use of the ISS "Mock" IT Infrastructure and Virtualized Server Farm.

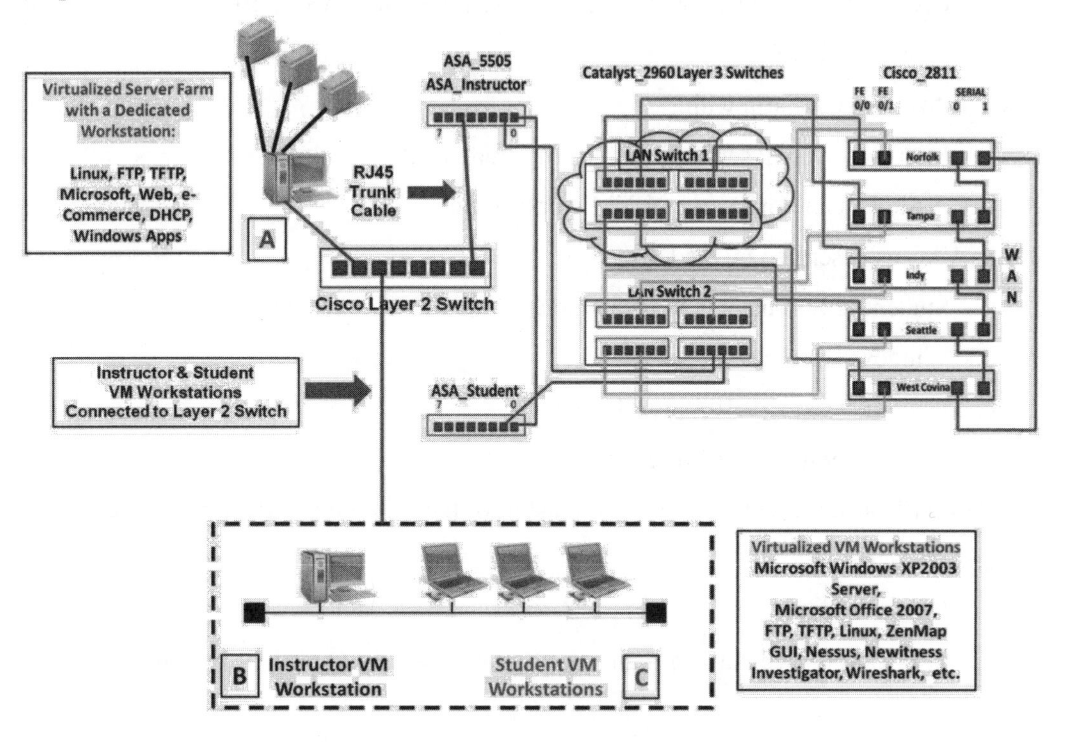

Figure 1 – ISS Onsite "Mock" IT Infrastructure & Virtualized Server Farm

The "Mock" IT Infrastructure and Virtualized Server Farm is a preconfigured IP network infrastructure complete with a classroom Cisco WAN and a virtualized server farm. All IP addressing schema, VLAN configurations, and layer 3 switching is preconfigured. The IP networking infrastructure remains static and only needs the following removable parts:

A) A classroom workstation (with at least 4 Gig RAM) capable of supporting an insert-able hard drive or USB hard drive with a pre-configured, virtualized server farm. This classroom workstation/server will support the virtualized server farm connected to the ASA_Instructor VLAN
B) An instructor workstation (with at least 2 Gig RAM) that shall act as the instructor's demonstration LAB workstation. The instructor will display the instructor workstation on the LCD projector to demonstrate the loading and configuring of the ISS "Mock" IT Infrastructure and Server Farm with VMware Player
C) Students LAB workstations will use a local copy of the ISS "Mock" IT Infrastructure Server Farm on a local or USB hard drive with VMware Player to run their Student and Target VMs

The following summarizes the setup, configuration, and equipment needed to perform Lab #2:

1. Standard ITT "Mock" IT Infrastructure and Virtualized Server Farm configuration and setup
    a. Cisco 2801 routers, 2960 catalyst LAN switches, and ASA 5505 firewalls with OSPF core and VLANs
2. A Virtualized Server Farm with:
    a. Microsoft DHCP server for allocating student IP host addresses
    b. A Student and/or Instructor VM workstation
3. Target VMs as described by the Lab:
    a. Student or Instructor VM with Nessus® and ZenMap installed
    b. Windows 2003 Server Target
    c. Ubuntu Desktop 9.10 Linux Target
    d. Ubuntu Server 10.04 Linux Target
4. Standard ITT onsite student workstation must have the following software applications loaded to perform this lab:
    a. VMware Player 3.x
    b. Microsoft Office 2007 or higher for Lab Assessment Questions & Answers

Nessus® v4.2.2 Vulnerability Assessment & Scanning Software

Training: Nessus® and Network Scanning Curriculums

If your information security teaching/training organization uses Nessus® in your curriculum to teach students how to scan for network vulnerabilities, the Tenable license allows you to use the HomeFeed subscription for your training purposes and may be found in Tenable's HomeFeed and ProfessionalFeed Subscription Agreement.

Program Rights, Requirements and Limitations:

You are permitted to copy/build images and redistribute Tenable's Nessus® and Tenable HomeFeed Plugins to students in/for the classroom setting only. Upon completion of the class, the ability to use the Plugins provided by the HomeFeed is terminated, and the students must re-register for either a HomeFeed or a ProfessionalFeed according to their intended use as is governed by the Subscription Agreement.

Information security organizations and the students are not permitted to use the HomeFeed in a commercial fashion to secure their organization's or a third party networks. It is only to be used for demonstration and teaching purposes in structured class environment.

If you qualify for the right to use a Tenable subscription for your teaching/training organization, you are required to review the license agreement in its entirety.
You will have the authorization to use the Nessus® logo in your presentation of the class(es). If you choose to use the Nessus® logo, it must always be accompanied by the following: "Nessus® is a Registered Trademark of Tenable Network Security, Inc."

Tenable reserves the right to revoke a free subscription or terminate a subscription at its sole discretion at any time.

Nessus® Overview

Nessus® performs remote scans and audits of Unix, Windows, and network infrastructures. Nessus® can perform a network discovery of devices, operating systems, applications, databases, and services running on those devices.

Any non-compliant hosts running applications such as peer-to-peer, spyware or malware (worms, Trojans, etc.) are detected and identified. Nessus® is capable of scanning all ports on every device and issuing remediation strategy suggestions as required.

Nessus® includes the ability to perform in-depth web application audits that identify vulnerabilities in custom built applications. Custom web applications can have their operating system, application, and SQL database audited and hardened against a variety of industry best practices and recommendations.

Recommended Procedures

Hands-on Lab #2 – Student Steps:

The following presents the steps needed to perform this vulnerability assessment scan on the targeted IP subnetwork and VM server farm:

1. Connect your student removable hard drive to your workstation
2. Boot up the Student VM and Microsoft DHCP VM server to allocate an IP host address
3. Enable your DOS command prompt and type "ipconfig" and "ping" your allocated IP host address 172.30.0.__ , the DHCP server 172.30.0.10, and the IP default gateway router 172.30.0.1
4. Login to your Instructor VM workstation and obtain an IP host address from the DHCP server connected to the layer 2 switch

NOTE: If the workstations in your physical classroom have only 2GB of RAM then only two VMs can be powered-on at once. For this lab, all you need to power-up is the "Student" VM workstation.

Run ZenMap GUI (Nmap) and Perform an IP Discovery and IP Host Scan

1. Click and enable ZenMap GUI from the Instructor VM desktop
2. Insert the target IP subnetwork number of 172.30.0.0/24 into the Nmap Target IP address field (Refer to Figure 3)
3. Select "Intense Scan" from the drop-down menu to the right of the Target IP address field (Refer to Figure 3)

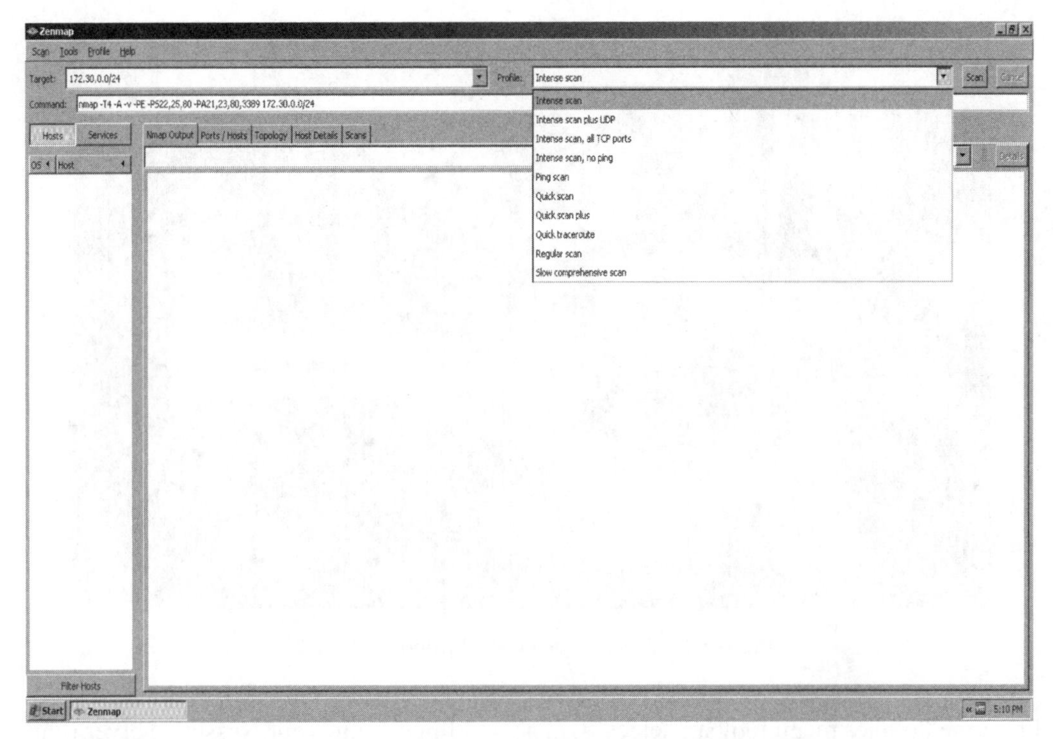

Figure 3 – ZenGUI Nmap Target IP Address & "Intense Scan" Dropdown Menu

4. Click on "Start Scan" to perform the "Intense Scan" on the Targeted IP subnetwork
5. The instructor will run the "Intense Scan" while projecting the real-time results of the tests on the overhead projector for the students to see and ask questions
6. Upon completion of the "Intense Scan" using ZenMap GUI (Nmap) as a reconnaissance and probing tool, the instructor will review the output created by the Nmap scan

Run Nessus® and Perform a Vulnerability Assessment Scan

1. Load the Nessus® v4.2.2.2 Server Manager on the Instructor VM
2. Connect to the Nessus® v4.2.2.2 Server Manager via an HTTPS:// secured browser connection as follows: https:// [IP host address]:8834/ in the navigation bar (at your Instructor VM DOS prompt, type "ipconfig" to display your IP host address
3. Login to the Nessus® Server Manager via your secure browser connection and authenticate

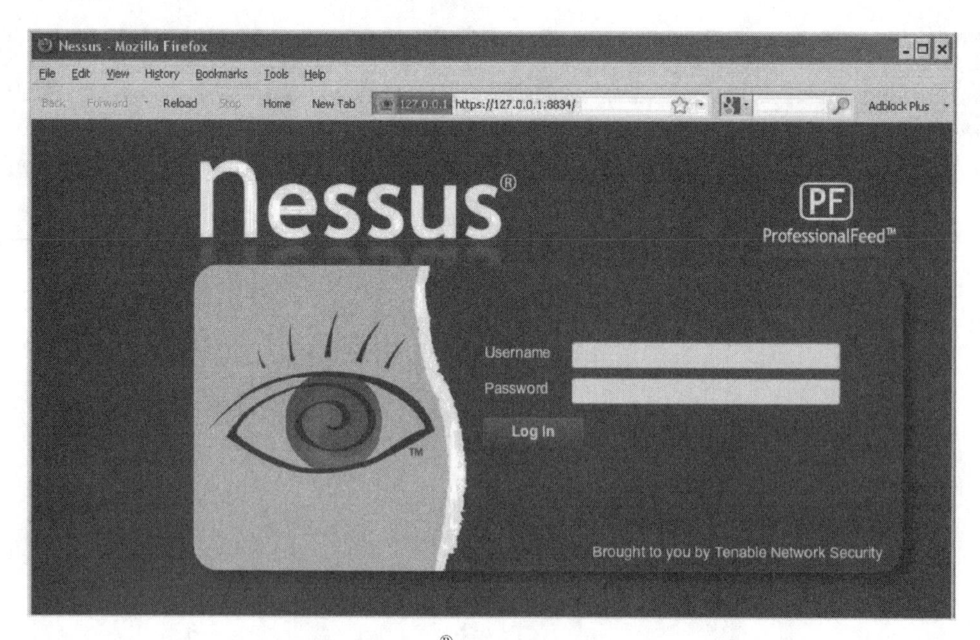

Figure 4 – Nessus® Server Manager v4.2.2.2

4. From the Policies menu toolbar, select "Lab 4" and Import into your Nessus® Server Manager. If there is no "Lab 4" policy definition – click on "Policies" and create a new "IT255 Lab 2 Policy" definition as follows:
    a. Click on Policies +Add
    b. Create a New Policy Definition: "IT255 Lab 2 Policy"
    c. Select all the Default Values in the "IT255 Lab 2 Policy" Definition
    d. Save the "IT255 Lab 2 Policy" Definition Using the Default Values
5. After loading a policy, you can create a new scan by clicking on the "**Scans**" option on the menu bar at the top and then click on the "**+ Add**" button on the right. The "**Add Scan**" screen will be displayed as follows:

Figure 5 – Nessus® Server Manager Add Policy Menu

6. There are five fields to enter the scan target:

   - **Name** – Sets the name that will be displayed in the Nessus® UI to identify the scan.

     Add Name: ***IT255 Lab #2 Server Farm Scan***

   - **Type** – Choose between "Run Now" (immediately execute the scan after submitting) or "Template" (save as a template for repeat scanning).

     Choose: ***Run Now***

   - **Policy** – Select a previously created policy that the scan will use to set parameters controlling Nessus server scanning behavior.

     Choose: ***IT255 Lab 2 Policy***

   - **Scan Targets** – Targets can be entered by single IP address (e.g., 192.168.0.1), IP range (e.g., 192.168.0.1-192.168.0.255), subnet with CIDR notation (e.g., 192.168.0.0/24) or resolvable host (e.g., www.nessus.org).

     Insert: **X.X.X.X – X.X.X.X or X.X.X.X/24.** Enter the IP subnetwork number of the ASA_Instructor VLAN where the server farm resides: 172.30.0.0/24.

   - **Targets File** – A text file with a list of hosts can be imported by clicking on "**Browse...**" and selecting a file from the local machine.

     Example host file formats and individual hosts:

     192.168.0.100, 192.168.0.101, 192.168.0.102

     Host range: 192.168.0.100-192.168.0.102

     Host CIDR block: 192.168.0.1/24

7. After you have entered the scan information, click on "**Submit**". After submitting, the scan will begin immediately before the display is returned to the general "**Scans**" page.

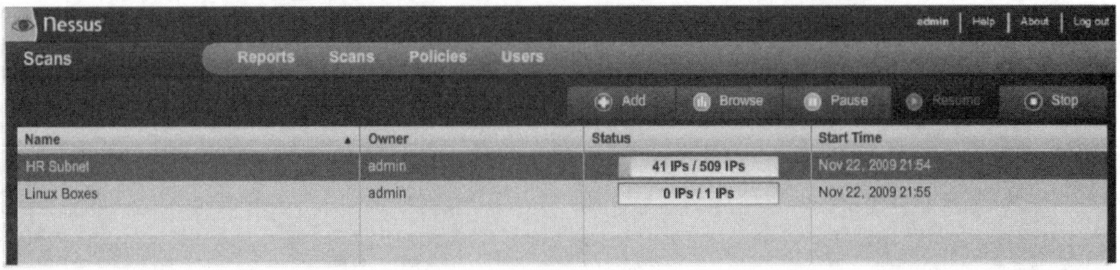

Figure 6 – Nessus® Server Manager Scans Page

8. Once a scan has launched, the Scans list will display a list of all scans currently running or paused along with basic information about the scan. After selecting a particular scan on the list, the action buttons on the top right allow you to "**Browse**" the results of the scan in progress, "**Pause**" and "**Resume**" the scan or "**Stop**" the scan completely.

9. When a scan has completed, it will be removed from the "**Scans**" list and be available for review on the "**Reports**" tab.

10. Clicking on the "Reports" tab on the menu bar at the top of the interface will bring up the list of running and completed scans. The "Reports" screen acts as a central point for viewing, comparing, uploading and downloading scan results.

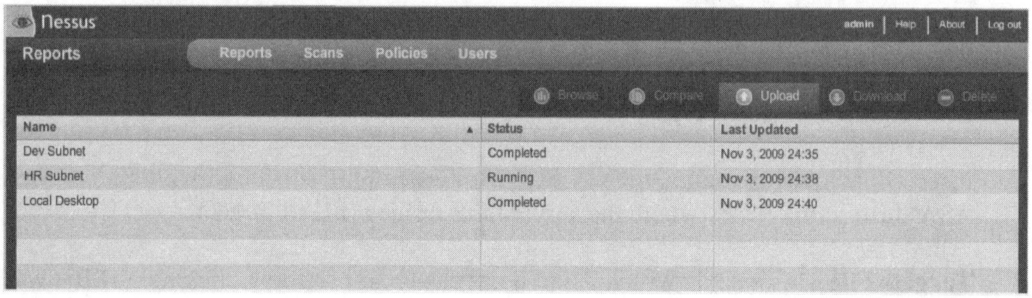

nessus — admin | Help | About | Log out

Reports — Reports Scans Policies Users

Browse Compare Upload Download Delete

Name	Status	Last Updated
Dev Subnet	Completed	Nov 3, 2009 24:35
HR Subnet	Running	Nov 3, 2009 24:38
Local Desktop	Completed	Nov 3, 2009 24:40

Figure 7 – Nessus® Server Manager Reports Page

11. To browse the results of a scan, select a name from the "Reports" list and click on "Browse". This allows you to view results by navigating through hosts, ports and then specific vulnerabilities. The first summary screen shows each host scanned along with a breakdown of vulnerabilities and open ports:

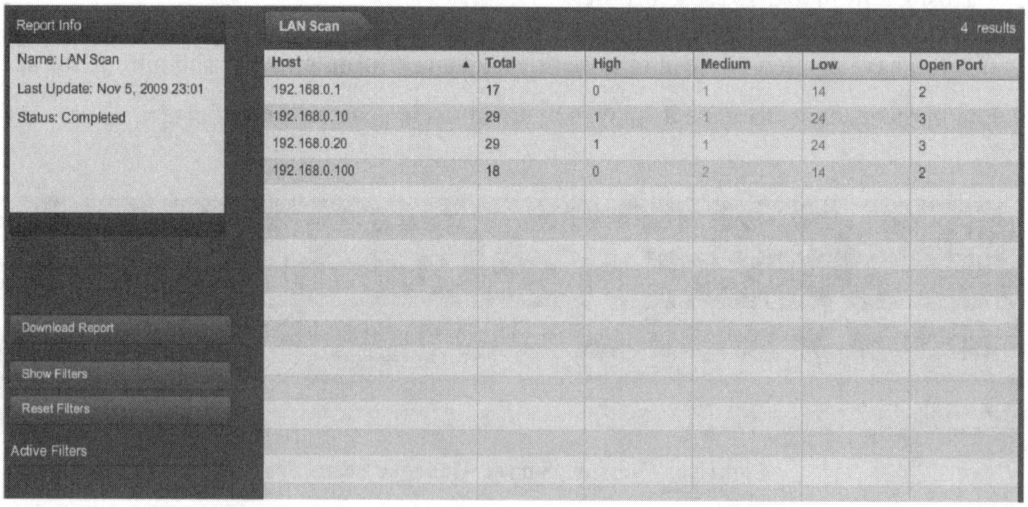

Report Info

Name: LAN Scan
Last Update: Nov 5, 2009 23:01
Status: Completed

Download Report
Show Filters
Reset Filters
Active Filters

LAN Scan — 4 results

Host	Total	High	Medium	Low	Open Port
192.168.0.1	17	0	1	14	2
192.168.0.10	29	1	1	24	3
192.168.0.20	29	1	1	24	3
192.168.0.100	18	0	2	14	2

Figure 8 – Nessus® Server Manager Reports Page

12. With a host selected, port number will segregate the report and display associated information such as the protocol and service name, as well as a summary of vulnerabilities categorized by risk severity. As you navigate through the scan results, the user interface will maintain the list of hosts as well as a series of clickable arrows to assist in quick navigation to a specific component of the report:

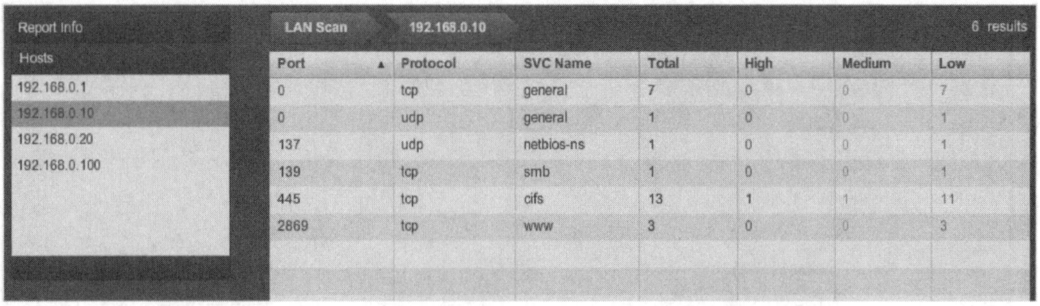

Report Info
Hosts
192.168.0.1
192.168.0.10
192.168.0.20
192.168.0.100

LAN Scan 192.168.0.10 6 results

Port	Protocol	SVC Name	Total	High	Medium	Low
0	tcp	general	7	0	0	7
0	udp	general	1	0	0	1
137	udp	netbios-ns	1	0	0	1
139	tcp	smb	1	0	0	1
445	tcp	cifs	13	1	1	11
2869	tcp	www	3	0	0	3

Figure 9 – Nessus® Server Manager Host Scan Report Results

13. Selecting a port will display all of the vulnerability findings associated with the port and service. In the example below, we see that host 192.168.0.10 has 13 vulnerabilities associated with TCP port 445 (CIFS or Common Internet File System). The summary of findings displays the Nessus Plugin ID, vulnerability name, port, protocol and severity.

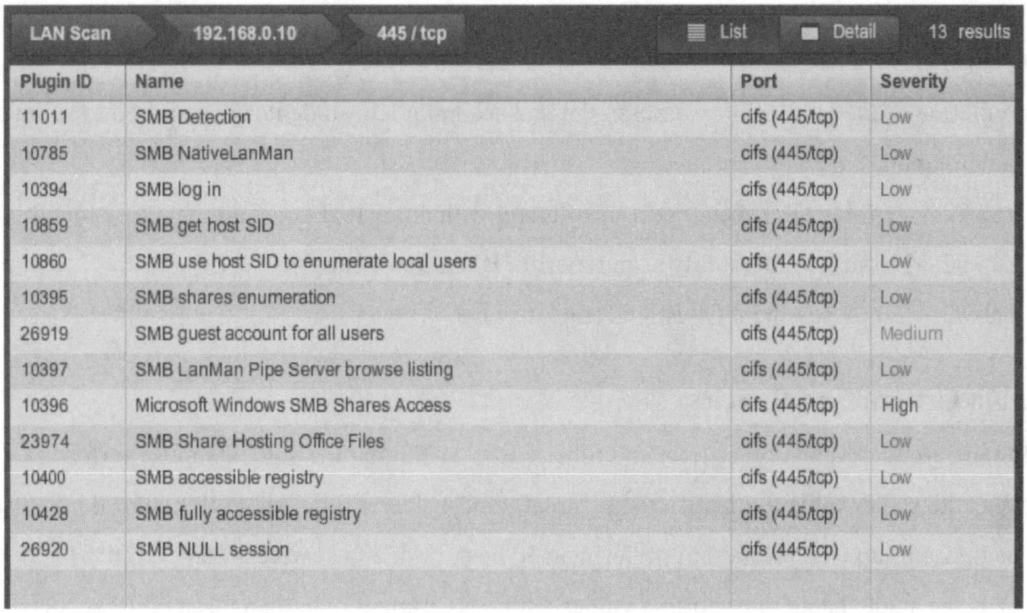

LAN Scan 192.168.0.10 445 / tcp List Detail 13 results

Plugin ID	Name	Port	Severity
11011	SMB Detection	cifs (445/tcp)	Low
10785	SMB NativeLanMan	cifs (445/tcp)	Low
10394	SMB log in	cifs (445/tcp)	Low
10859	SMB get host SID	cifs (445/tcp)	Low
10860	SMB use host SID to enumerate local users	cifs (445/tcp)	Low
10395	SMB shares enumeration	cifs (445/tcp)	Low
26919	SMB guest account for all users	cifs (445/tcp)	Medium
10397	SMB LanMan Pipe Server browse listing	cifs (445/tcp)	Low
10396	Microsoft Windows SMB Shares Access	cifs (445/tcp)	High
23974	SMB Share Hosting Office Files	cifs (445/tcp)	Low
10400	SMB accessible registry	cifs (445/tcp)	Low
10428	SMB fully accessible registry	cifs (445/tcp)	Low
26920	SMB NULL session	cifs (445/tcp)	Low

Figure 10 – Nessus® Server Manager Host Scan Vulnerability Findings

By clicking once on any column heading, the results can be sorted by the column's content. Clicking a second time will reverse sort the results:

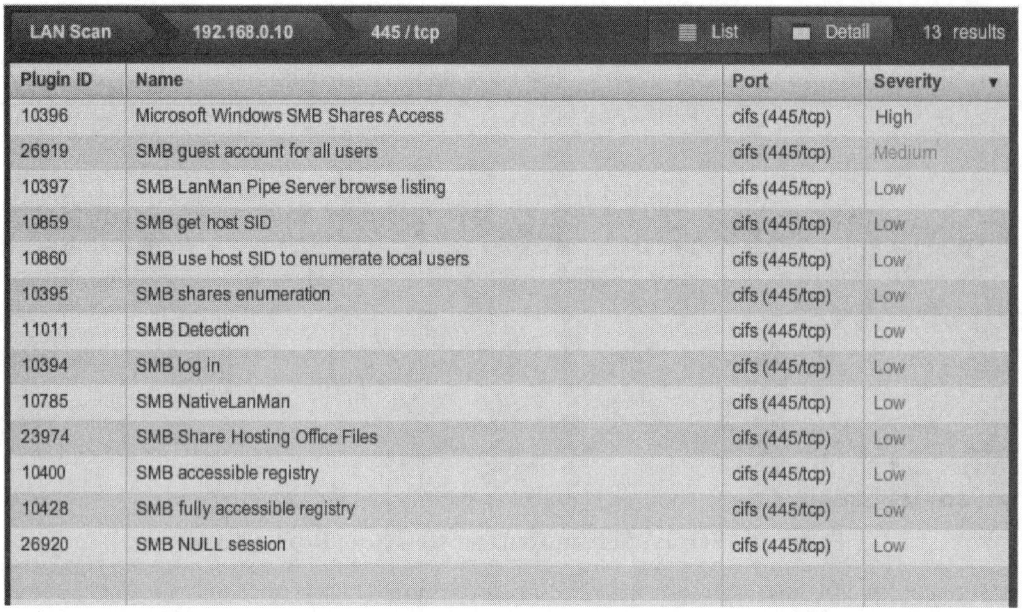

LAN Scan	192.168.0.10	445 / tcp	List Detail 13 results
Plugin ID	**Name**	**Port**	**Severity ▼**
10396	Microsoft Windows SMB Shares Access	cifs (445/tcp)	High
26919	SMB guest account for all users	cifs (445/tcp)	Medium
10397	SMB LanMan Pipe Server browse listing	cifs (445/tcp)	Low
10859	SMB get host SID	cifs (445/tcp)	Low
10860	SMB use host SID to enumerate local users	cifs (445/tcp)	Low
10395	SMB shares enumeration	cifs (445/tcp)	Low
11011	SMB Detection	cifs (445/tcp)	Low
10394	SMB log in	cifs (445/tcp)	Low
10785	SMB NativeLanMan	cifs (445/tcp)	Low
23974	SMB Share Hosting Office Files	cifs (445/tcp)	Low
10400	SMB accessible registry	cifs (445/tcp)	Low
10428	SMB fully accessible registry	cifs (445/tcp)	Low
26920	SMB NULL session	cifs (445/tcp)	Low

Figure 11 – Nessus® Server Manager Host Scan Sorted Vulnerability Findings

14. Selecting a vulnerability from the list will display full details of the finding including a technical description, references, solution, detailed risk factor and any relevant output demonstrating the finding:

Deliverables

Upon completion of the vulnerability assessment and scanning lab, students are required to submit the following deliverables:

1. Lab #2 – ZenMap GUI scan report in softcopy with annotated notes on what was found
2. Lab #2 – Nessus® vulnerability scan report in HTML soft copy
3. Lab #2 – Lab Assessment Questions and Answers

Evaluation Criteria and Rubrics

The following are the evaluation criteria and rubrics for Lab #2 that the students must perform:

1. Was the student able to identify risks, threats, and vulnerabilities in an IP network infrastructure using ZenMap GUI (Nmap) to perform an IP host, port, and services scan? – [**20%**]
2. Was the student able to perform a vulnerability assessment scan on a targeted IP subnetwork using Nessus®? – [**20%**]

3. Was the student able to compare the results of the ZenMap GUI "Intense Scan" with a Nessus® vulnerability assessment scan and make a distinction? – [**20%**]
4. Was the student able to assess the findings of the vulnerability assessment scan and identify critical vulnerabilities? – [**20%**]
5. Was the student able to make recommendations for mitigating the identified risks, threats, and vulnerabilities as described by the CVE listing for the found vulnerabilities? – [**20%**]

Lab #2 – Assessment Worksheet

Perform a Vulnerability Assessment Scan Using Nessus®

Course Name & Number: ______________________________

Student Name: ______________________________

Instructor Name: ______________________________

LAB Due Date: ______________________________

Overview

This lab demonstrates the first 3 steps in the hacking process that is typically performed when conducting ethical hacking or penetration testing. The first step in the hacking process is to perform an IP host discovery and port/services scan (Step 1: Reconnaissance & Probing) on a targeted IP subnetwork using ZenMap GUI (Nmap) security scanning software. The second step in the hacking process is to perform a vulnerability assessment scan (Step 2: Scanning) on the targeted IP subnetwork using Nessus® vulnerability assessment scanning software. Finally, the third step in the hacking process (Step 3: Enumeration) is to identify information pertinent to the vulnerabilities found in order to exploit the vulnerability.

Lab Assessment Questions & Answers

1. What is the application ZenMap GUI typically used for? Describe a scenario in which you would use this type of application.

2. What is the relationship between risks, threats and vulnerabilities as it pertains to Information Systems Security throughout the seven domains of a typical IT infrastructure?

3. Which application is used for Step #2 in the hacking process to perform a vulnerability assessment scan?

4. Before you conduct an ethical hacking process or penetration test on a live production network, what must you do prior to performing the reconnaissance and probing and scanning procedures?

5. What is a CVE listing? Who hosts and who sponsors the CVE database listing website?

6. Can ZenMap GUI detect what operating systems are present on IP servers and workstations? What would that option look like in the command line if running a scan on 172.30.0.10?

7. If you have scanned a live host and detected that it is running Windows XP workstation OS, how would you use this information for performing a Nessus® vulnerability assessment scan?

8. Once a vulnerability is identified by Nessus®, where can you check for more information regarding the identified vulnerability, exploits, and the risk mitigation solution?

9. What is the major different between ZenMap GUI and Nessus®?

10. Why do you need to run both ZenMap GUI and Nessus® to perform the first 3 steps of the hacking process?

Laboratory #3

Lab #3: Enable Windows Active Directory and User Access Controls

Learning Objectives and Outcomes

Upon completing this lab, students will be able to complete the following tasks:

- Design a Windows Active Directory and User access control framework
- Create a new Windows Active Directory domain controller
- Evaluate existing user and group permission rights in Active Directory user accounts and their workstations
- Create new Windows Active Directory users and groups with custom permission rights
- Create and verify access control lists to protect objects and folders from unauthorized access

Required Setup and Tools

This lab does not require the use of the ISS Mock IT Infrastructure - Cisco core backbone network. In addition, the Instructor VM workstation and Student VM workstations should be physically disconnected from the ITT internal network and be isolated on a dedicated layer 2 switch. This will allow for a shared DHCP server to be used to allocate the IP addresses for the instructor and student workstations. The following are **required** for this hands-on lab:

A) A classroom workstation (with at least 2 Gig RAM) capable of supporting an insert-able hard drive or USB hard drive with a pre-configured virtualized server farm. This classroom workstation/server will support the virtualized server farm connected to the ASA_Instructor VLAN

B) An instructor workstation (with at least 2 Gig RAM) that shall act as the instructor's demonstration LAB workstation. The instructor will display the Instructor workstation on the LCD projector to demonstrate the loading and configuring of the ITT "Mock" IT Infrastructure and Server Farm with VMware Player

C) Students LAB workstations will use a local copy of the ITT "Mock" IT Infrastructure Server Farm on a local or USB hard drive with VMware Player to run their Student and Target VMs

The following summarizes the setup, configuration, and equipment needed to perform Lab #3:

1. A Virtualized Server Farm with the following components:
    a. Microsoft DHCP server for allocating student IP host addresses
    b. A Student and/or Instructor VM workstation

2. Target VMs as described by the Lab:
   a. "WindowsTarget01" Server
      i. Roles that will be installed: Active Directory Services and DNS Server
   b. Administrator account access on "WindowsTarget01" VM Server
      - Windows Server 2003 Standard Edition 32-bit (VM Name: "TargetWindows01")
        - Computer Name: Windows02
        - Three Users Available: administrator, instructor or student (case sensitive)
        - Password: ISS316Security
        - IP Address: DHCP
        - Domain Login: NO
   c. Administrator account access on the Student VM Workstation
3. Standard ITT onsite student workstation must have the following software applications loaded to perform this lab:
   a. VMware Player 3.x
   b. Microsoft Office 2007 or higher for Lab Assessment Questions & Answers

Recommended Procedures

Hands-on Lab #3 – Student Steps:

To perform this hands-on lab, students are required to perform the following steps:

1. Connect the student-removable hard drive to your workstation.
2. Boot up the Instructor VM and Microsoft DHCP VM server to allocate an IP host address.
3. Enable your DOS command prompt and type "ipconfig" and "ping" your allocated IP host address 172.30.0.__ , the DHCP server 172.30.0.10, and the IP default gateway router 172.30.0.1.
4. Login to your Instructor VM workstation and obtain an IP host address from the DHCP server connected to the layer 2 switch.

NOTE: If the workstations in your physical classroom have only 2GB of RAM then only two VMs can be powered-on at once. You can power-on 2 VMs at once "WindowsDHCP01" and "TargetWindows01" to maximize performance or you can load the "WindowsDHCP01" VM server in a separate workstation connected to the classroom layer 2 switch. This will provide you with the ability to load the "Student" VM workstation and the "TargetWindows01" VM server in the same physical workstation.

5. Login into the "WindowsTarget01" VM server as "administrator".
6. On the "WindowsTarget01" VM click Start > Run > and type into the command prompt: **dcpromo**

7. Answer all the necessary questions to create a New Active Directory Forest enabling DNS and reboot.
8. Log into "WindowsTarget01" as an administrator of the new domain.
9. Create the following global domain user accounts and groups using Active Directory Users and Computers (Start -> Administrative Tools -> Active Directory Users and Computers):
   a. ShopFloor group
   b. HumanResources group
   c. Manager group
   d. 'SFuser01' user account (use 'SFuser01pass' for the password) – member of ShopFloor group
   e. 'SFmanager' user account (use 'SFmanagerpass' for the password) – member of ShopFloor and Manager groups
   f. 'HRuser01' user account (use 'HRuser01pass' for the password) – member of HumanResources group
   g. 'Manager01' user account (use 'Manager01pass' for the password) – member of HumanResources and Manager groups
10. Create four new folders:
    a. C:\ERPdocuments – This folder will contain miscellaneous shared files for the ERP software
    b. C:\ERPdocuments\HRfiles – Folder for shared Human Resources (HR) user files
    c. C:\ERPdocuments\SFfiles – Folder for shared Shop Floor (SF) user files
    d. C:\ERPdocuments\MGRfiles – Folder for shared Manager user files
11. Determine what type of access controls are needed to allow the following actions:
    a. Allow Shop Floor users to read and write files in C:\ ERPdocuments\SFfiles.
    b. Allow Human Resources users to read and write files in C:\ ERPdocuments\HRfiles.
    c. Manager01 users to read and write files in C:\ ERPdocuments\MGRfiles and C:\ ERPdocuments\HRfiles.
12. Perform the following steps to evaluate the effectiveness of your access controls:
    a. Log in as SFuser01.
    b. Use notepad to create a new text file, lab1file.txt, in C:\ERPdocuments\SFfiles.
    c. Attempt to create a new text file, lab1file.txt, in C:\ERPdocuments\HRfiles.
    d. Log in as HRuser01.
    e. Use notepad to create a new text file, lab2file.txt, in C:\ERPdocuments\HRfiles.
    f. Attempt to create a new text file, lab2file.txt, in C:\ERPdocuments\SFfiles.

13. Login as Manager01 and verify that you can read and write files in C:\ERPdocuments\HRfiles and C:\ERPdocuments\MGRfile, but not C:\ERPdocuments\SFfiles.

Deliverables

Upon completion of Lab #3: Enable Windows Active Directory and User Access Controls, students are required to provide the following deliverables:

1. Lab #3 – Text file outlining the Active Directory Tree created
2. Lab #3 – Lab Assessment Questions & Answers

Evaluation Criteria and Rubrics

The following are the evaluation criteria and rubrics for Lab #3 that the students must perform:

1. Was the student able to design a Windows Active Directory and User access control framework? – **[20%]**
2. Was the student able to create a new Windows Active Directory domain controller definition? – **[20%]**
3. Was the student able to evaluate existing user and group permission rights in Active Directory user accounts and their workstations? – **[20%]**
4. Was the student able to create new Windows Active Directory users and groups with custom permission rights for user accounts and folders? – **[20%]**
5. Was the student able to create and verify access control lists to protect objects and folders from unauthorized access? – **[20%]**

Lab #3 – Assessment Worksheet

Enable Windows Active Directory and User Access Controls

Course Name & Number: ______________________________

Student Name: ______________________________

Instructor Name: ______________________________

LAB Due Date: ______________________________

Overview

This lab provides students with the hands-on skills needed to create a new Active Directory domain in Windows Server 2003 and demonstrates how to configure a centralized authentication and policy definition for access controls. The Active Directory users and workstation plug-ins will be used to create users, groups, and configure role-based access permissions and controls on objects and folders in a Windows Server 2003 Active Directory system.

Lab Assessment Questions & Answers

1. What are the three fundamental elements of an effective access control solution for information systems?

2. What two access controls can be setup for a Windows Server 2003 folders and authentication?

3. If you can browse a file on a Windows network share but are not able to copy it or modify it what type of access controls and permissions are probably configured? What type of Access Control would best describe this access control situation?

4. What is the mechanism on a Windows Server where you can administer granular policies and permissions on a Windows network using role-based access?

5. What is two-factor authentication and why is it an effective access control technique?

6. Relate how Windows Server 2008 R2 Active Directory and the configuration of access controls achieve C-I-A for departmental LANs, departmental folders, and data.

7. Is it a good practice to include the account or user name in the password? Why or why not?
8. Can a user who is defined in the Active Directory access a shared drive if that user is not part of the domain?
9. Does Windows Server 2003 require a user's login/password credentials prior to accessing shared drives?
10. When granting access to LAN systems for GUESTS (i.e., auditors, consultants, third-party individuals, etc.), what security controls do you recommend be implemented in order to maximize C-I-A of production systems and data?

Laboratory #4

Lab #4: Configure Group Policy Objects and Microsoft Baseline Security Analyzer (MBSA)

Learning Objectives and Outcomes

Upon the completion of this lab, the students will be able to conduct the following tasks:

- Define Active Directory Group Policy Objects (GPO) in Windows 2003 Server
- Deploy GPOs to domain workstations within Windows 2003 Server
- Configure login credentials and specify password requirements and parameters for domain workstations within Windows 2003 Server
- Use Microsoft Baseline Security Analyzer (MBSA) to security baseline a Windows 2003 Server and Windows XP Professional Workstation
- Enable automatic and online security updating and patching from Microsoft's web servers via the Internet for Windows 2003 Server and Windows XP Professional Workstation

Required Setup and Tools

This lab does not require the use of the ISS Mock IT Infrastructure - Cisco core backbone network. In addition, the Instructor VM workstation and Student VM workstations should be physically disconnected from the ITT internal network and be isolated on a dedicated layer 2 switch. This will allow for a shared DHCP server to be used to allocate the IP addresses for the instructor and student workstations. The following are **required** for this hands-on lab:

A) A classroom workstation (with at least 2 Gig RAM) capable of supporting an insert-able hard drive or USB hard drive with a pre-configured, virtualized server farm. This classroom workstation/server will support the virtualized server farm connected to the layer 2 switch for all VM workstations

B) An instructor workstation (with at least 2 Gig RAM) that shall act as the Instructor's demo LAB workstation. The instructor will display the workstation on the LCD projector to demo the loading and configuring of the Windows Server 2003 VM GPOs and MBSA

C) Students' lab workstations will use a local copy of the ITT "Mock" IT Infrastructure VM server farm contained on their removable hard drive to run their Student VM and "WindowsTarget01" VM server

Password GPO GPO Security Policy Test GPO
- 15 Security Type Settings
MBSA Run.

The following summarizes the setup, configuration, and equipment needed to perform Lab #4:

1. A Virtualized Server Farm with the following comonents:
    a. Microsoft DHCP server for allocating student IP host addresses
    b. A Student and/or Instructor VM workstation
2. "TargetWindows01" VM as needed for this lab:
    a. Windows 2003 Server Target with MBSA 2.1.1 installed
    b. Administrator account access on the Windows 2003 Target VM Server
    c. Administrator account access Student VM Workstation
        - Windows Server 2003 Standard Edition 32-bit (VM Name: "TargetWindows01")
            - Computer Name: Windows02
            - Three Users Available: administrator, instructor or student (case sensitive)
            - Password: ISS316Security
            - IP Address: DHCP
            - Domain Login: NO
3. Standard ITT ISS onsite student workstation must have the following software applications loaded to perform this lab:
    a. VMware Player 3.x
    b. Microsoft Office 2007 or higher for Lab Assessment Questions & Answers

Recommended Procedures

Hands-on Lab#4 – Student Steps:

To perform this hands-on lab, students are required to perform the following steps:

1. Connect the student-removable hard drive to your workstation.
2. Boot up the Instructor VM and Microsoft DHCP VM server to allocate an IP host address.
3. Enable your DOS command prompt and type "ipconfig" and "ping" your allocated IP host. address 172.30.0.__ , the DHCP server 172.30.0.10, and the IP default gateway router 172.30.0.1.
4. Login to your Student VM workstation and obtain an IP host address from the DHCP server connected to the layer 2 switch.

NOTE: If the workstations in your physical classroom have only 2GB of RAM then only two VMs can be powered-on at once. You can power-on 2 VMs at once "WindowsDHCP01" and "TargetWindows01" to maximize performance or you can load the "WindowsDHCP01" VM server in a separate workstation connected to the classroom layer 2 switch. This will provide you with the ability to load the "Student" VM workstation and the "TargetWindows01" VM server in the same physical workstation.

5. Login into the Student VM and Windows01 Target VM.
6. Launch Active Directory Users and Computers on Windows01: Start -> Administrative Tools -> Active Directory Users and Computers.
7. In the tree view, expand Forest -> Domains -> domainname -> right click Properties.
8. Select 'Group Policy Objects,' open the context menu, (right-mouse-click on Group Policy Objects), select 'New'.
9. Enter 'PasswordGPO' for the name and select 'OK'.
10. Open the context menu of the newly created GPO and select 'Edit…'.
11. In the Group Policy Management Editor treeview, expand Computer Configuration -> Policies -> Windows Settings -> Security Settings -> Account policies. Select 'Password Policy'.
12. Double-click 'Password must meet complexity requirements,' and choose Enable. Choose 'OK'.
13. Double-click 'Minimum Password Length' and enter 8. Choose 'OK'.

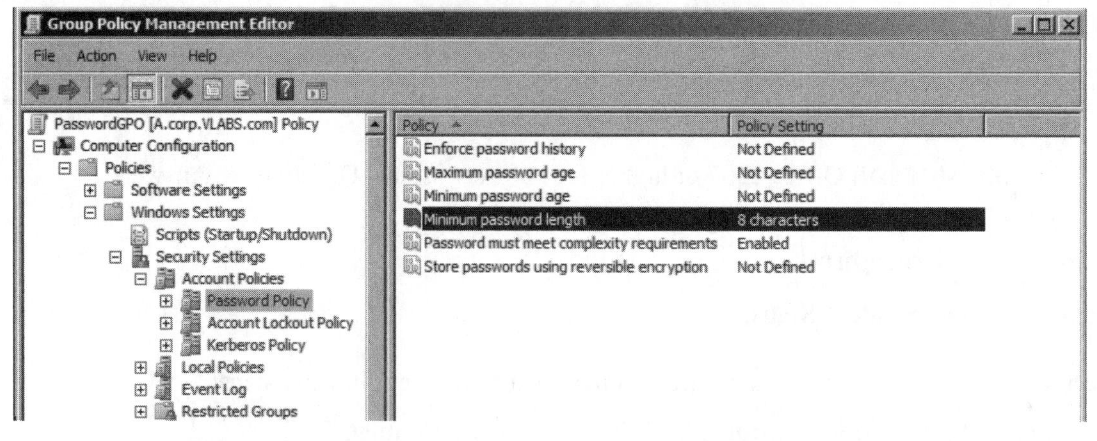

Figure 12 –Microsoft Windows Group Policy Management Editor

14. Close the Group Policy Management Editor.
15. Open the context menu for the domain, and select 'Link an Existing GPO…"
16. Select 'PasswordGPO,' and choose 'OK'.
17. Open the context menu for 'PasswordGPO,' and choose 'Save Report'. Enter the desired filename and folder to save the 'PasswordGPO' report.
18. Launch MBSA from the Windows Server 2003 desktop.
19. Select 'Scan a computer'.
20. Remove the check mark from "Check for security updates" if the system does not have internet access.
21. Choose 'Start Scan'.

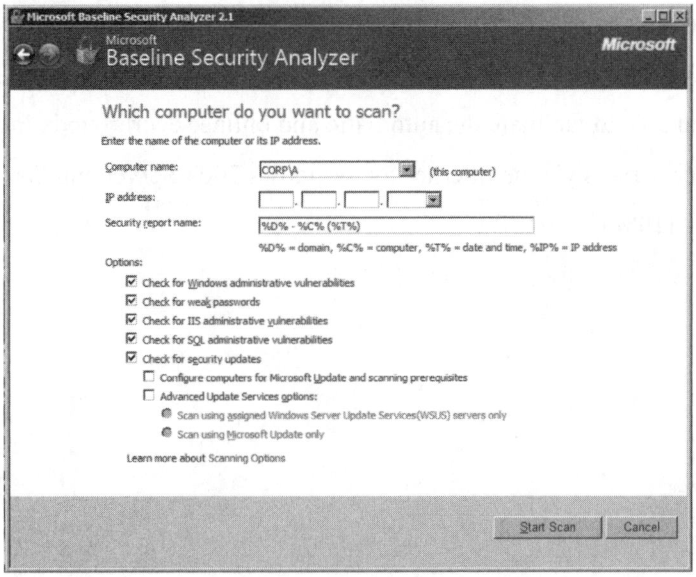

Figure 13 –Microsoft Windows Baseline Security Analyzer

22. When the scan is complete, select 'Copy to clipboard' to save the output to the clipboard.
23. Open Notepad, paste the clipboard contents, and save the MBSA scan results and submit as part of your Lab #4 deliverables.

Deliverables

Upon completion of the Group Policy Objects and MBSA lab, students are required to provide the following deliverables:

1. Lab #4 – Soft copy of your GPO report for the GPO created in this lab in HTML format
2. Lab #4 – A Word document that contains the results of the MBSA scan
3. Lab #4 – Assessment Questions & Answers

Evaluation Criteria and Rubrics

The following are the evaluation criteria and rubrics for Lab #4 that the students must perform:

1. Was the student able to define Active Directory Group Policy Objects (GPO) in Windows 2003 Server? – [**20%**]
2. Was the student able to deploy GPOs to domain workstations within Windows 2003 Server? – [**20%**]
3. Was the student able to configure login credentials and specify password requirements and parameters for domain workstations within Windows 2003 Server? – [**20%**]

4. Was the student able to use Microsoft Baseline Security Analyzer (MBSA) to security baseline a Windows 2003 Server and Windows XP Professional Workstation? – [**20%**]
5. Was the student able to facilitate the automatic and online security updating and patching from Microsoft's web servers via the Internet for Windows 2003 Server and Windows XP Professional Workstation? – [**20%**]

Lab #4 – Assessment Worksheet

Configure Group Policy Objects and Microsoft Baseline Security Analyzer (MBSA)

Course Name & Number: ______________________________

Student Name: ______________________________

Instructor Name: ______________________________

LAB Due Date: ______________________________

Overview

During this lab the students will use Group Policy Objects to create a Minimum Password Length Password Policy and link it to the newly created domain from the previous lab. They will also be running the Microsoft Security Baseline Analyze (MBSA) and discussing the results of the MBSA scan with the class.

Lab Assessment Questions & Answers

1. Define why change control management is relevant to security operations in an organization?
2. What type of access control system uses security labels?
3. Describe two options you would enable in a Window's Domain password policy?
4. Where would patch management and software updates fall under in security operations and management?
5. Is there a setting in your GPO to specify how many login attempts will lockout an account? Name 2 parameters that you can set to enhance the access control to the system.
6. What are some Password Policy parameter options you can define for GPOs that can enhance the C-I-A for system access?
7. What sources could you use as a source to perform the MBSA security state?
8. What does WSUS stand for, and what does it do?

9. What is the difference between MBSA and Microsoft Update?

10. What are some of the options that you can exercise when using the MBSA tool?

Laboratory #5

Lab #5: Perform Protocol Capture & Analysis Using Wireshark & Netwitness Investigator

Learning Objectives and Outcomes

Upon completing this lab, students will be able to:

- Use Wireshare & Netwitness Investigator as a packet capture and protocol analysis tool
- Capture live IP, ICMP, TCP and UDP traffic using TELNET, FTP, TFTP, and SSH sessions
- Examine captured packet traces to view clear-text and cipher-text
- Analyze the packet capture data in Netwitness Investigator and be able to identify the difference between UDP and TCP sessions
- Identify common network related protocols used for client-server communications, network management and network security

Required Setup and Tools

This lab requires the use of the ISS "Mock" IT Infrastructure and Virtualized Server Farm. This is shown below:

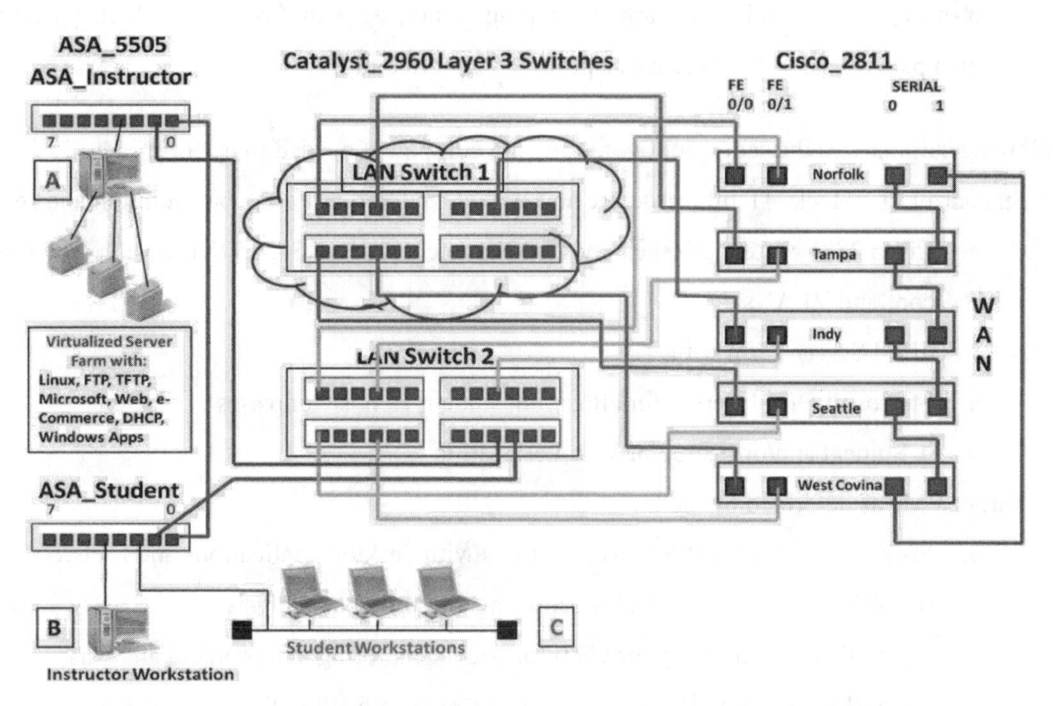

Figure 1 – ISS Onsite "Mock" IT Infrastructure & Virtualized Server Farm

The "Mock" IT Infrastructure and Virtualized Server Farm is a preconfigured, IP network infrastructure complete with a classroom Cisco WAN and a virtualized server farm. All IP addressing schema, VLAN configurations, and layer 3 switching is preconfigured. The IP networking infrastructure remains static and only needs the following removable parts:

A) A classroom workstation (with at least 4 Gig RAM) capable of supporting an insert-able hard drive or USB hard drive with a preconfigured, virtualized server farm. This classroom workstation will support the virtualized VM server farm connected to the classroom layer 2 switch and the connection to ASA_Instructor

B) An instructor VM workstation (with at least 2 Gig RAM) that shall act as the demonstration traffic generator for the protocol capture of hands-on labs. The Instructor will engage ARP, DHCP, ICMP, TCP 3-way handshake, FTP, HTTP, TELNET, and SSH to demonstrate protocol interaction from a preconfigured Instructor Virtual Machine (VM). The Instructor workstation connects to the same layer 2 switch and then to the ASA_Instructor

C) Student VM workstations (with at least 2 Gig RAM) use a preconfigured Student VM to act as an Attacker VM as well as a traffic monitoring and protocol capture device. Since all the Student VM workstations are connected to the same layer 2 switch, students can perform the protocol interaction lab (i.e., arp, dhcp, ping, telnet, ssh, tftp, ftp, etc.) while they capture their own packets using Wireshark as a protocol capture tool

The following summarizes the setup, configuration, and equipment needed to perform Lab #5:

1. Standard ITT "Mock" IT Infrastructure and Virtualized Server Farm configuration and setup
   a. Cisco 2801 routers, 2960 catalyst LAN switches, and ASA 5505 firewalls with OSPF core and VLANs
2. A Virtualized Server Farm with:
   a. Microsoft DHCP server for allocating student IP host addresses
   b. A Student and/or Instructor VM workstation
3. Target VMs as described by the Lab:
   a. Instructor and Student VM workstations with desktop applications and tools:
      - Wireshark 1.2.9 for packet capturing and protocol analysis
      - NetWitness Investigator v 9.0 for packet capturing and protocol analysis
      - TELNET and SSH open source client software – PuTTY
      - FTP and TFTP open source client software – FileZilla and TFTPd32
      - Adobe Reader for PDF Documentation

4. Standard ISS onsite student workstation must have the following software applications loaded to perform this lab:
    a. VMware Player 3.x
    b. Microsoft Office 2007 or higher for Lab Assessment Questions & Answers

Recommended Procedures

Hands-on Lab #5 – Student Steps:

To perform this hands-on lab, students are required to perform the following steps:

1. Connect the instructor removable hard drive to your workstation
2. Boot up the Instructor VM and Microsoft DHCP VM server to allocate an IP host address
3. Connect the Instructor VM workstation to the LCD overhead projector for classroom display
4. Enable your DOS command prompt and type "**ipconfig**" and "**ping**" your allocated IP host address 172.30.0.__ , the DHCP server 172.30.0.10, and the IP default gateway router 172.30.0.1
5. Login to your Instructor VM workstation and obtain an IP host address from the DHCP server connected to the layer 2 switch:

    Login ID: "**instructor**" or "**student**" (case sensitive)

    Password: "**ISS316Security**" (case sensitive)

NOTE: If the workstations in your physical classroom have only 2GB of RAM then only two VMs can be powered-on at once. You have to split the VM server farm into 2 physical workstations, loading 2 VM servers in each ("WindowsDHCP01" and "TargetWindows01") and ("TargetUbuntu01" and "TargetUbuntu02") to maximize performance.

6. Power-up in VMware Player, the "TargetWindows01" VM server and logon using the provided credentials:

    Windows 2003 Server Standard Edition

    - Windows Server 2003 Standard Edition 32-bit (VM Name: "TargetWindows01")
        - Computer Name: Windows02
        - Three Users Available: administrator, instructor or student (case sensitive)
        - Password: ISS316Security
        - IP Address: DHCP
        - Domain Login: NO

    - FTP (Filezilla FTP Server)
        - Port: 21
        - Username: instructor or student
        - Password: <blank>

- TFTP (Tftpd32 TFTP Server)
  - Port: 69
  - Username: <none>
  - Password: <blank>

7. Power-up the VMware Player, the "TargetUbuntu01" VM server and SSH logon using the provided credential:

   Ubuntu Server Target VM - TargetUbuntu01

- Ubuntu Linux 10.04 LTS Server (VM Name: "TargetUbuntu01")
  - Computer Name: Ubuntu01
  - **ONE** User available ONLY in v1: administrator <case sensitive>
  - Three Users available in v2: administrator, student or instructor <case sensitive>
  - Password: ISS316Security (case sensitive)
  - IP Address: eth0 set to DHCP, eth1 and eth2 not set.

- SSH
  - Port: 21
  - Username: administrator <case sensitive>
  - Password: ISS316Security (case sensitive)

- Apache running "Damn Vulnerable Web App" (DVWA)
  - URL: http://<serveripaddress>/dvwa
  - Password: password
  - Username: admin

8. Identify the target network device IP addresses from the following chart:

ISS Mock IT Infrastructure IP Addresses					
Router Name	**Serial 0/0**	**Serial 0/1**	**Fastethernet 0/0**	**Fastethernet 0/1**	**Loopback 0**
R1.WEST COVINA	172.19.0.2/30	172.20.0.1/30	172.20.8.1/24	172.20.20.1/24	172.20.1.1/32
Description	R1.SEATTLE-S 0/1	R1.NORFOLK-S 0/1	DMZ-LAN-SW1-FE0/16	TRUST-LAN-SW2-FE0/16	
Router Name	**Serial 0/0**	**Serial 0/1**	**Fastethernet 0/0**	**Fastethernet 0/1**	**Loopback 0**
R1.SEATTLE	172.18.0.2/30	172.19.0.1/30	172.19.8.1/24	172.19.20.1/24	172.19.1.1/32
Description	R1.INDY-S 0/1	R1.WESTCOVINA-S 0/0	DMZ-LAN-SW1-F0/2-V400	TRUST-LAN-SW2-F0/2-V401	
Router Name	**Serial 0/0**	**Serial 0/1**	**Fastethernet 0/0**	**Fastethernet 0/1**	**Loopback 0**
R1.INDY	172.17.0.2/30	172.18.0.1/30	172.18.8.1/24	172.18.20.1/24	172.18.1.1/32
Description	R1.TAMPA-S 0/1	R1.SEATTLE-S 0/0	DMZ-LAN-SW1-F0/17-V300	TRUST-LAN-SW2-F0/17-V301	
Router Name	**Serial 0/0**	**Serial 0/1**	**Fastethernet 0/0**	**Fastethernet 0/1**	**Loopback 0**
R1.TAMPA	172.16.0.2/30	172.17.0.1/30	172.17.8.1/24	172.17.20.1/24	172.17.1.1/32
Description	R1.NORFOLK-S 0/1	R1.INDY-S 0/0	DMZ-LAN-SW1-F0/7-V200	TRUST-LAN-SW2-F0/7-V201	
Router Name	**Serial 0/0**	**Serial 0/1**	**Fastethernet 0/0**	**Fastethernet 0/1**	**Loopback 0**
R1.NORFOLK	172.20.0.2/30	172.16.0.1/30	172.16.8.1/24	172.16.20.1/24	172.16.1.1/32
Description	R1.WEST COVINA-S 0/1	R1.TAMPA-S 0/0	DMZ-LAN-SW1-FE0/1	TRUST-LAN-SW2-FE0/1	
Switch Name	**Vlan 100**	**Fastethernet 0/1**	**Fastethernet 0/2**	**Fastethernet 0/7**	**Fastethernet 0/8**
LAN.SW1	172.16.8.5/24				
Description		R1.NORFOLK-F 0/0	R1.SEATTLE-F 0/0	R1.TAMPA-F0/0	R1.WEST COVINA-F0/0
Switch Name	**Vlan 101**	**Fastethernet 0/1**	**Fastethernet 0/2**	**Fastethernet 0/7**	**Fastethernet 0/8**
LAN.SW2	172.16.20.5/24				
Description		R1.NORFOLK-F 0/1	R1.SEATTLE-F 0/1	R1.TAMPA-F0/1	R1.WEST COVINA-F0/1
ASA Name	**Vlan2 "Inside"**	**Vlan501 "Outside"**	**Vlan600 "DMZ"**		
ASA-Student	172.31.0.1/24 (IP Default GW)	172.20.20.10/24	172.29.0.2/24		
Description	Can only ping this from vlan2.	Can ping this from outside.	Cannot ping this from outside.		
ASA Name	**Vlan2 "Inside"**	**Vlan501 "Outside"**	**Vlan600 "DMZ"**		
ASA-Instructor	172.30.0.1/24 (IP Default GW)	172.20.20.11/24	172.29.0.1/24		
Description	Can ony ping this from vlan2.	Can ping this from outside.	Cannot ping this from outside.		

9. Load Wireshark and start a packet capture in promiscuous mode while you perform the various traffic generating tasks
10. From your DOS command prompt, make sure you can ping the destination IP address before you attempt to TELNET, SSH, TFTP, or FTP to the destination host as follows:

    Ping 172.30.0.___ (your IP host address allocated by the DHCP server)

    Ping 172.30.0.10 (the DHCP server)

    Ping 172.30.0.1 (the IP default gateway router)

    Ping 172.X.X.X (where 172.X.X.X = IP destination address – refer to IP Address Chart in Step 8)
11. Run the PuTTY application from the Instructor VM workstation and enter the targeted IP addresses for your TELNET and SSH exercise:
    a. TELNET to LAN Switch 1 and enter the userid and password of "cisco" / "cisco"
    b. TELNET to Indy and enter the userid and password of "cisco" / "cisco"

c. TELNET to Tampa and enter the userid and password of "cisco" / "cisco"

d. SSH to LAN Switch 2 (only for 2960s that support SSH) and enter the userid and password of "cisco" / "cisco"

e. SSH to the "TargetUbuntu01" VM server (172.30.0.X – check the DHCP server for the IP host address or ask the Instructor what the IP host address is) and enter the SSH (port 21) login credentials:

   - Port: 21
   - Username: administrator <case sensitive>
   - Password: ISS316Security (case sensitive)

f. SSH to WestCovina (if SSH is enabled) and enter the userid and password of "cisco" / "cisco"

g. Click on TFTPd32 on your desktop and load client on your student VM workstation. TFTP a small file from your Student VM workstation to the TFTPd32 Server on the "TargetWindows01" VM server (172.30.0.X – ask your instructor for the allocated IP host address of the "TargetWindows01" VM server)

h. Click on Filezilla FTP on your desktop and load the client FTP application on your student VM workstation. FTP a small file from our Student VM workstation to the FileZilla FTP server on the "TargetWindows01" VM server (172.30.0.X – ask your instructor for the allocated IP host address of the "TargetWindows01" VM server)

12. "Stop Capture" in Wireshark and save the file as "IT255 Lab #5.pcap" and submit as part of your lab deliverables – review the protocol to decode, and answer the Lab #5 assessment questions
13. Import the IT255 Lab #5.pcap file into Netwitness Investigator by first creating a new local connection called "IT255 Lab #5.pcap. Then import the *.pcap file into Netwitness Investigator for further protocol analysis

Deliverables

Upon completion of the packet capture and protocol analysis, students are required to provide the following deliverables as part of this lab:

1. Lab #5 – Wireshark Protocol Capture File – IT255 Lab #5.pcap
2. Lab #5 – Submit a screenshot of the imported *.pcap file into Netwitness Investigator (Print Screen – Copy Paste into a WORD document).
3. Lab #5 – Lab Assessment Questions & Answers

Evaluation Criteria and Rubrics

The following are the evaluation criteria and rubrics for Lab #5 that the students must perform:

- Was the student able to use Wireshare & Netwitness Investigator as a packet capture and protocol analysis tool? – [**20%**]
- Was the student able to capture live IP, ICMP, TCP and UDP traffic using TELNET, FTP, TFTP, and SSH sessions and distinguish them? – [**20%**]
- Was the student able to examine captured packet traces to view clear-text and cipher-text data? – **[20%]**
- Was the student able to analyze the packet capture data in Wireshark or Netwitness Investigator and be able to identify the difference between UDP and TCP sessions? – [**20%**]
- Was the student able to identify common network-related protocols used for client-server communications, network management and network security? – [**20%**]

Lab #5 – Assessment Worksheet

Perform Protocol Capture & Analysis Using Wireshark & Netwitness Investigator

Course Name & Number: ______________________________

Student Name: ______________________________

Instructor Name: ______________________________

LAB Due Date: ______________________________

Overview

One of the most important tools needed for information systems security practitioners is a packet capture and protocol analysis tool. Wireshark is a freeware tool providing basic packet capture and protocol decoding capabilities. NetWitness Investigator is a free and commercial solution (free version allows up to twenty 1GB Collections of packet captures) that provides security practitioners with a deep packet inspection tool used for examining everything from the data link layer up to the application layer. NetWitness Investigator is the only protocol analysis tool that provides deep packet inspection and advanced decoding for simplified full packet capture and session analysis.

LAB Assessment Questions & Answers

1. What is the purpose of the address resolution protocol (ARP)?

2. What is the purpose of the dynamic host control protocol (DHCP)?

3. What was the DHCP allocated source IP host address for the Student VM and Target VM?

4. When you pinged the targeted IP host, what was the source IP address and destination IP address of the ICMP echo-request packet?

5. Did the targeted IP host respond to the ICMP echo-request packet with an ICMP echo-reply packet? If yes, how many ICMP echo-request packets were sent back to the IP source?

6. Find a TCP 3-way handshake for a TELNET, FTP, or SSH session. What is the significance of the TCP 3-way handshake?

7. What was the SEQ# of the initial SYN TCP packet and ACK# of the SYN ACK TCP packet?

8. During the Instructor's TELNET session to LAN Switch 1 and LAN Switch 2 – what was the captured terminal password for LAN Switch 1 and LAN Switch 2?

9. When the Instructor used SSH to a Cisco router, were you able to see the terminal password? Why or why not?

10. What other IP packets are on the VLAN and Ethernet LAN segment? How can these other IP packets provide additional clues or information about the logical IP routing and IP addressing schema?

Laboratory #6

Lab #6: Perform Business Continuity Plan Implementation Planning

Learning Objectives and Outcomes

Upon completing this lab, students will be able to complete the following tasks:

- Identify the major elements of a Business Continuity Plan (BCP) and requirements for a fictitious organization
- Perform a high-level Business Impact Analysis (BIA) and Risk Analysis (RA) for a fictitious organization
- Prioritize from the BIA and RA business functions and processes that must be part of the business continuity plan
- Craft a BCP plan outline that addresses the BIA and RA and business priorities
- Define the necessary BCP implementation planning steps that include testing, practice, and documentation maintenance of back-up and recovery procedures

Required Setup and Tools

This is a paper-based, hands-on lab and does not require the use of the ISS "Mock" IT infrastructure or Virtualized Server Farm.

The following summarizes the setup, configuration, and equipment needed to perform Lab #6:

1. Standard ITT onsite student workstation must have the following software applications loaded to perform this lab:
    a. Microsoft Office 2007 or higher for Lab Assessment Questions & Answers and for crafting a BCP outline, BIA, and RA priorities
    b. Fictitious organization business functions and processes spreadsheet

Recommended Procedures

Hands-on Lab #6 – Student Steps:

The instructor will lead the following classroom discussion to set the stage for the fictitious organization's Business Continuity Planning requirements.

1. Review the fictitious organization's business functions and processes
2. Distinguish between an RA and BIA, and a BCP and DRP
3. Align the RA and BIA as the foundation for priorities for your BCP and DRP
4. Assess business drivers for prioritization of the BCP and DRP business functions and processes

5. Discuss what the process would be to perform an RA and BIA
    a. Develop information gathering questionnaires
    b. Conduct interviews and one-on-one meetings with business leaders and departmental managers of critical business functions and operations
    c. Align business drivers with key business functions and processes
    d. Prioritize the business' critical business functions and processes
    e. Identify the IT systems, applications, and data that support the prioritized business functions and processes
    f. Assess the financial impact that these critical business functions and processes have on the business
6. Define the key business continuity metrics that drive the overall business continuity plan
    a. Business risk analysis and business impact analysis prioritization of critical business functions and processes
    b. Recovery Time Objectives (RTO) for critical business functions and processes
    c. Financial loss versus cost of recovery impact analysis
7. Discuss how to define the scope of the BCP and how that scope can be narrowed based on mission critical priorities and financial budgets
8. Discuss how business asset replacement insurance can impact the cost and investment of business continuity solutions
9. Review the major components of a business continuity plan:
    a. BCP Policy
    b. BCP Organizational Structure
    c. Business Impact Analysis
    d. IT Systems, Applications, & Data
    e. BCP Drivers & Priorities
    f. BCP Scope and Objectives
    g. Business Functions & Processes Back-Up & Recovery
    h. BCP Testing & Plan Updating
    i. BCP Maintenance & On-Going Management
10. Review the elements of a BCP implementation plan
    a. Initiating the BCP
    b. Back-Up and Recovery Procedures for IT Systems, Applications, & Data
    c. Key BCP Personnel and Organizational Structure

d. Prepare Key Documents, Tools, and Instructions for Recovery
e. Handling Emergencies or Disaster Recovery Situations
f. Manage Business Recovery
g. Perform Business Recovery Steps
h. Test the BCP
i. Train IT and Departmental Personnel on Business Recovery and Back-Up Procedures
j. Maintain and Update the BCP

Deliverables

Upon completion of this paper-based lab, students are required to submit the following deliverables:

1. Lab #6 – Completed Business Recovery Strategy Assessment Spreadsheet
2. Lab #6 – Create a BCP Plan Outline and Implementation Plan Outline for the Fictitious Organization
3. Lab #6 – Lab Assessment Questions & Answers

Evaluation Criteria and Rubrics

The following are the evaluation criteria and rubrics for Lab #6 - Perform Business Continuity Plan Implementation Planning:

1. Was the student able to identify the major elements of a Business Continuity Plan (BCP) and requirements for a fictitious organization? – [**20%**]
2. Was the student able to perform a high-level Business Impact Analysis (BIA) and Risk Analysis (RA) for a fictitious organization? – [**20%**]
3. Was the student able to prioritize from the BIA and RA business functions and processes that must be part of the business continuity plan? – [**20%**]
4. Was the student able to craft a BCP plan outline that addresses the BIA and RA and business priorities? –[**20%**]
5. Was the student able to define the necessary BCP implementation planning steps that include testing, practice, and documentation of back-up and recovery procedures –[**20%**]

Lab #6 – Business Recovery Strategy Assessment Spreadsheet
e-Commerce/e-Business Organization

List of Key Business Functions & Processes

- E-commerce processes – primary revenue source for the organization
- E-mail based communications – internal for business communications and external for customer service
- Telephone call center and on-line customer services – enhanced e-customer service delivery with call center and self-service customer website
- Manufacturing and production line – just in time inventory and distribution of products
- Production processes – just in time manufacturing and integrated supply chain
- Quality control mechanisms – maximize product quality
- Maintenance and support services – keep production lines open
- Sales and sales administration – inside sales, online sales, sales support, resellers and distributors, etc.
- Finance and accounting – G/L, A/R, A/P, Payroll, Benefits
- Research and development activities – product development
- Human resources management – employee services
- Information technology services & Internet connectivity – supports e-commerce and e-business infrastructure
- Premises (Head Office and branches) – headquarters facility and administration office
- Marketing and public relations – internet marketing and branding

Lab #6 – Business Recovery Strategy Assessment Spreadsheet
e-Commerce/e-Business Organization

List of Impacted IT Systems, Applications, & Data

Business Function or Process	Priority	IT Systems, Applications & Data
➢ E-mail based communications	10	POP3, SMTP Mail Servers
➢ Website and e-commerce website (Payroll for HR)	1	Web Server, e-Commerce Server, (Manual Payroll Processing or External)
➢ Telephone call center	3	VoIP Telephony Infrastructure
➢ Customer service	4	Customer Server System / CRM
➢ Manufacturing and production line	7	Automation System & Manufacturing
➢ Production processes	8	Production Scheduling System
➢ Quality control mechanisms	12	QC System
➢ Maintenance and support services	14	Maintenance & Support System
➢ Sales and sales administration	6	Sales Order Entry, Sales Support
➢ Finance and accounting	9	GL, A/R, A/P Accounting System
➢ Research and development activities	17	R&D System
➢ Human resources management	15	HR, Employment, Benefits
➢ Information technology services	2	7-Domains of Typical IT Infrastructure (Website/Internet/Online)
➢ Internet connectivity & telephone service	5	Broadband Internet, VoIP System
➢ Premises (Head Office and branches)	13	HQ LAN/VoIP/IT Infrastructure
➢ Marketing and public relations	16	Marketing Analysis System

Lab #6 – Assessment Worksheet

Perform Business Continuity Plan Implementation Planning

Course Name & Number: ________________________________

Student Name: ________________________________

Instructor Name: ________________________________

LAB Due Date: ________________________________

Overview

The instructor will lead the class in discussions pertaining to a business continuity plan. Key elements of a business continuity plan starting with a risk analysis, business impact analysis, and alignment of critical business functions and processes will be discussed. Students will craft a business continuity implementation plan outline as part of this lab's deliverables.

Lab Assessment Questions & Answers

1. What is the different between a risk analysis (RA) and a business impact analysis (BIA)?
2. What is the difference between a Disaster Recovery Plan and a Business Continuity Plan?
3. Typically, a business continuity plan is also a compilation or collection of other plans. What other plans might a BCP and all supporting documents include?
4. What is the main difference between a Disaster Recovery Plan (DRP) and a Business Continuity Plan (BCP)?
5. What is the purpose of a risk assessment and business impact analysis? Why is this an important first step in defining a BCP and DRP?
6. How does risk assessment (RA) relate to a business impact analysis for an organization?
7. Given the list of identified mission critical business functions and processes, what kind of company would you say this organization is, and what do you think are its most important business processes and functions?

8. Given the prioritization list provided for the organization's identified business functions and processes, write an assessment of how this prioritization will impact the need for IT systems, applications, and data access.

9. For the top 5 identified business functions and processes, what recovery time objective (RTO) would you recommend for this organization and why?

10. Why is payroll for employees and Human Resources listed as a co-number 1 business priority?

Laboratory #7

Lab #7: Relate Windows Encryption and Hashing to Confidentiality & Integrity

Learning Objectives and Outcomes

Upon completing this lab, students will be able to:

- Apply the concepts of using common cryptographic and encryption techniques to ensure confidentiality
- Apply the concepts of hashing to ensure integrity of data transmission and data reception
- Identify the output of common cryptographic and hashing tools on transmitted data and verity confidentiality and integrity
- Implement an MD5 sum or SHA1 hash on a data transmission or message to verify data transmission integrity
- Implement GPG for Windows to encrypt a data message to ensure confidentiality

Required Setup and Tools

This lab does not require the use of the ISS Mock IT Infrastructure - Cisco core backbone network. In addition, the Instructor VM workstation and Student VM workstations should be physically disconnected from the ITT internal network and be isolated on a dedicated layer 2 switch. This will allow for a shared DHCP server to be used to allocate the IP addresses for the instructor and student workstations. The following is required for this hands-on lab:

A) A classroom workstation (with at least 4 Gig RAM) capable of supporting an insert-able hard drive or USB hard drive with a pre-configured, virtualized server farm. This classroom workstation will support the virtualized server farm connected to the classroom layer 2 switch

B) An instructor workstation (with at least 2 Gig RAM) that shall act as the Instructor's demo LAB workstation. The instructor will display the Instructor workstation on the LCD projector to demo the loading and configuring of the Instructor VM Workstation and VM Server Farm with VMware Player

C) Students LAB workstations will enable their own Student VM and VM Server Farm to run the Target VMs

The following summarizes the setup, configuration, and equipment needed to perform Lab #7:

1. The VM server farm with:
    a. The Microsoft "WindowsDHCP01" VM server enabled for allocating student IP host addresses
    b. The Instructor VM for the instructor and the Student VM for the students
2. Target VMs as described by the Lab:
    a. Windows 2003 Server "TargetWindows01" VM server
    b. Instructor and Student VM with GPG installed
3. Standard ITT onsite student workstation must have the following software applications loaded to perform this lab:
    a. VMware Player 3.x
    b. Microsoft Office 2007 or higher for Lab Assessment Questions & Answers

Recommended Procedures

Hands-on Lab #7 – Student Steps:

To perform this hands-on lab, students are required to perform the following steps:

1. Connect the student-removable hard drive to your workstation
2. Boot up the Student VM and Microsoft DHCP VM server to allocate an IP host address
3. Connect the Student VM workstation to the LCD overhead projector for classroom display
4. Enable your DOS command prompt and type "**ipconfig**" and "**ping**" your allocated IP host address 172.30.0.59, the DHCP server 172.30.0.10, and the IP default gateway router 172.30.0.1
5. Login to your Instructor VM workstation and obtain an IP host address from the DHCP server connected to the layer 2 switch:
   Login ID: "**student**" (case sensitive)
   Password: "**ISS316Security**" (case sensitive)

NOTE: If the workstations in your physical classroom have only 2GB of RAM then only two VMs can be powered-on at once. You can load your Instructor VM and the "TargetWindows01" VM server simultaneously. Obtain an IP host address from the DHCP server connected to the same layer 2 classroom switch to maximize performance.

6. Power-up in VMware Player, the "TargetWindows01" VM server and logon using the provided credentials:

Windows 2003 Server Standard Edition

- Windows Server 2003 Standard Edition 32-bit (VM Name: "TargetWindows01")
  - Computer Name: Windows02
  - Three Users Available: administrator, instructor or student (case sensitive)
  - Password: ISS316Security
  - IP Address: DHCP
  - Domain Login: NO

- FTP (Filezilla FTP Server)
  - Port: 21
  - Username: instructor or student
  - Password: <blank>

- TFTP (Tftpd32 TFTP Server)
  - Port: 69
  - Username: <none>
  - Password: <blank>

7. GPG should already be pre-installed and located on the desktop of the Instructor VM workstation and the "TargetWindows01" VM server

> Note: If GPG is not on your desktop, look inside your \vlabs folder on the c:\ drive for the GPG install file. Install the GPG application with all the default installation configuration values.

8. Click on the GPG desktop icon to create your private key (Screen #1)
9. Insert the name "Student" as the name asked for. And click "Forward"
10. To create a unique private key, insert your individual email address, (student01@vlabsolutions.com) and click "Forward"
11. Create a backup copy of your new key when prompted and click "Forward"
12. Enter a passphrase to further encrypt your newly created key (this is your secret key). Write down this passphrase as it will be what needs to be used to decrypt and encrypt messages
13. After generation of your key, save it to the desktop for quick access
14. Click on close, and now open up GPG again. Highlight the key you just created, and click on the export option and name the key "StudentVM" as appropriate
15. Repeat steps 10-14 to create a public key for the "TargetWindow01" VM.
16. Click on the "TargetWinVM01" key, and click on the export option and name the key "TargetVM01"

17. Transfer both sets of keys to each of the VM's by copying, cutting, and pasting or use an external USB hard drive to ensure the public keys are transferred to both the Student VM and the "TargetWindows01" VM server
18. Use the GPG import button, and import the public keys to both VM's
19. On the Student VM right click newly imported key, and click on "Set Owner Trust" option, and set it to "Full" in the options selection
20. On the Student VM, right click newly imported key, and click on "Sign Keys" option, and enter your secret key passphrase from generation earlier to sign the public key to your secret key ring as authorized
21. For Hashing, we can verify the public key was imported correctly into both the Student VM workstation and the "TargetWindows01" VM server. Integrity is maintained if the hash value matches the Fingerprint in the GPG home window
22. On the Student VM, create a new file on the desktop using notepad, and name the file IT255 Lab #7.txt, and add a message in the text file "I like information systems security"
23. Save the IT255 Lab #7.txt file and right click, and chose the "Sign and Encrypt" option. Make sure you check the "Remove Unencrypted File" option at the bottom (Refer to Screen #3)
24. Add both certificates (keys) to the "Options" and click "Encrypt"! (Refer to Screen #4)
25. Once encrypted, you will see the encrypted file replace the plain text file on the desktop, right click and choose decrypt/verify option (Refer to Screen #5)
26. Now transfer the encrypted file to the "TargetWindows01" VM server desktop, and perform the similar steps from Step #22 - #25 to decrypt (not encrypt) the file just received on "TargetWindows01" VM server

Deliverables

Upon completion of this lab, students are required to provide the following deliverables:

1. Lab #7 – Your original GPG encrypted message and decrypted message
2. Lab #7 – Your Hash value for the hashed file
3. Lab #7 – Lab Assessment Questions & Answers

Evaluation Criteria and Rubrics

The following are the evaluation criteria and rubrics for Lab #7: Relate Windows Encryption and Hashing to Confidentiality & Integrity:

1. Was the student able to apply the concepts of using common cryptographic and encryption techniques to ensure confidentiality? – **[20%]**
2. Was the student able to apply the concepts of hashing to ensure integrity of data transmission and data reception? – **[20%]**
3. Was the student able to identify the output of common cryptographic and hashing tools on transmitted data and verity confidentiality and integrity? – **[20%]**
4. Was the student able to implement an MD5 sum or SHA1 hash on a data transmission or message to verify data transmission integrity? – **[20%]**
5. Was the student able to implement GPG for Windows to encrypt a data message to ensure confidentiality? – **[20%]**

Lab #7 – Assessment Worksheet

Relate Windows Encryption and Hashing to Confidentiality & Integrity

Course Name & Number: ____

Student Name: ____

Instructor Name: ____

LAB Due Date: ____

Overview

This lab demonstrates how hashing tools can be used to ensure message and file transfer integrity and how encryption can be used to maximize confidentiality. Common hashing and encryption tools including MD5, SHA1, and GnuPG will be used. The students will engage in hashing exercises to demonstrate message and file integrity using both MD5 and SHA1 on their Student VM and "TargetWindows01" VM server desktop. They will execute the MD5 and SHA1 hashing tools on their Student VM desktop on a sample file comparing the hash value when the sample file is modified or altered. They will then load GnuPG to generate both a public and private key and a secret key for encryption only. The students will share public keys and the secret keys in order to send secure messages and files from the Student VM to the "TargetWindows01" VM server.

LAB Assessment Questions & Answers

1. Which Key do you provide anyone you want to encrypt messages with private or public keys or both?
2. What does GPG allow you to do once it is installed?
3. Name 2 different types of encryption supported by GPG for your key?
4. What happens when you sign and trust a new key to your keychain?
5. If a user sends you his public key will he be able to decrypt your encrypted messages once you import and sign his key?
6. What are the similarities between an MD5 hash and a fingerprint?
7. How would you encrypt a webserver and the pages it serves up?

8. Why is hashing all database inputs not considered encryption of the database? What value does hashing database entries from server to client?

9. Where would you remove a user's certificate from being able to access systems on your network?

10. Which connection type is secure and which is clear text between SSH, Telnet and FTP?

Laboratory #8

Lab #8: Perform a Website & Database Attack by Exploiting Identified Vulnerabilities

Learning Objectives and Outcomes

Upon completing this lab, students will be able to complete the following tasks:

- Identify web application and web server backend database vulnerabilities as viable attack vectors
- Develop an attack plan to compromise and exploit a web site using cross-site scripting (XSS) against sample vulnerable web applications
- Conduct a manual Cross-site Scripting (XSS) attack against sample vulnerable web applications
- Perform SQL injection attacks against sample vulnerable web applications with e-commerce data entry fields
- Mitigate known web application and web server vulnerabilities with security countermeasures to eliminate risk from compromise and exploitation

Required Setup and Tools

This lab does not require the use of the ISS Mock IT Infrastructure - Cisco core backbone network. In addition, the Instructor VM workstation and Student VM workstations should be physically disconnected from the ITT internal network and be isolated on a dedicated layer 2 switch. This will allow for a shared DHCP server to be used to allocate the IP addresses for the instructor and student workstations. The following is required for this hands-on lab:

A) NOT NEEDED - A classroom workstation/server (with at least 4 Gig RAM) capable of supporting the removable hard drive with the VM server farm.

B) An instructor workstation/server (with at least 2 Gig RAM/4Gig RAM recommended) that shall act as the Instructor's test bed for performing the demo lab. The instructor will power-on the "WindowsDHCP01" VM server, the "TargetUbuntu01" Linux VM server, and the Instructor VM workstation using VMware Player.

C) Students' Lab workstations will use their own VM server farm and VM student workstation. VMware Player will be used to run the Student VM and the Target VM.

The following summarizes the setup, configuration, and equipment needed to perform Lab #8:

1. A Virtualized Server Farm with:
   a. Microsoft DHCP server for allocating student IP host addresses
   b. Instructor VM workstation

2. Target VMs as described by the Lab:

   - Ubuntu Linux 10.04 LTS Server (VM Name: "TargetUbuntu01")
     - Computer Name: Ubuntu01
     - **ONE** User available ONLY: administrator <case sensitive>
     - Password: ISS316Security (case sensitive)
     - IP Address: eth0 set to DHCP, eth1 and eth2 not set.

   - SSH
     - Port: 21
     - Username: administrator <case sensitive>
     - Password: <blank>

   - Apache running "Damn Vulnerable Web App" (DVWA)
     - URL: http://<serveripaddress>/dvwa
     - Username: admin
     - Password: password

3. Standard ITT ISS onsite student workstation must have the following software applications loaded to perform this Lab:
   a. VMware Player
   b. Web Browser (Internet Explorer)
   c. Microsoft Office 2007 or higher for Lab Assessment Questions & Answers

Recommended Procedures

Hands-on Lab #8 – Student Steps:

Students should perform the following steps:

1. Connect your removable hard drive to your ITT student workstation and logon using GUEST credentials.

> Note: wait for the Instructor to disconnect the classroom workstations from the ITT internal network and live Internet prior to booting up your student VM workstation to obtain an IP host address from the DHCP server

2. Using VMware Player, power-up your student VM workstation and obtain an IP host address from the "WindowsDHCP01" server.
3. Using VMware Player, power-up your "TargetUbuntu01" Linux VM server and obtain an IP host address from the "WindowsDHCP01" server.

> Note: If you only have 2 Gig RAM, you may want to put static IP address configurations in your Student VM workstation and "TargetUbuntu01" Linux VM server so you don't have to power-on the "WindowsDHCP01" VM server. Once you have valid IP host addresses and can ping each other (Student VM and "TargetUbuntu01" Linux VM, you can now perform the web application and web server attacks on the "TargetUbuntu01" Linux VM server.

4. Log into the "TargetUbuntu01" Linux VM server and verify that it has received an IP address by typing:
   $ sudo ifconfig –a
5. If it has an IP host address, then connect to it using your Instructor VM workstation's Internet Explorer browser: http://targetubuntu01 IP host /dvwa
6. If it does not have an IP address, first verify which eth is being detected by the VM? i.e. eth0, eth1, eth2, etc…? This information is provided in the ifconfig command's output.
7. To set a static IP or to set a non-standard eth interface to DHCP on Ubuntu follow these steps:
   a. $ sudo nano /etc/network/interfaces
   b. Once the nano editor comes up enter the following entry for your particular eth interface (insert the **eth#** that is displayed as enabled on your VM – it may not be eth0, eth1, eth2, etc.):
      i. auto lo **eth0**
         iface lo inet loopback
         iface **eth0** inet static
         address 172.30.0.xxx(xxx= your static ip host address)
         netmask 255.255.255.0 (enter the /24 netmask)
         gateway 172.30.0.1 (enter the IP default gateway ip here)
   c. For DHCP enter the following:
      i. auto lo **eth0**
         iface lo inet loopback
         iface **eth0** inet dynamic
   d. Save and exit by hitting CTRL+X on the keyboard and Y to save the file.
   e. Type the following to restart:
      $ sudo /etc/init.d/networking restart

To Exploit a Cross-site Scripting (XSS) Vulnerability in DVWA perform the following:

1. Exploit a cross site scripting vulnerability to cause a message to appear on a user's screen.
2. Provide a screen shot or description of the attack
3. With "TargetUbuntu01" enabled, you need to open your Internet Explorer browser to connect to the web site:

> http://172.30.0.x/dvwa, where x is the IP host address allocated by the DHCP server
>
> - URL: http://<targetubunto01 IP host address>/dvwa
> - Username: admin
> - Password: password

4. Once the web page comes up, login and click on the DVWA Security tab and set it to low.
5. Click on the XSS Reflective tab which will display our vulnerable web application test "Reflective Cross Site Scripting" against the web site.
6. Try to insert in the provided input box the following:
   <this is a test!>
   See the output there. This indeed shows that we can further send scripts through the validation box provided.
7. Reflective XSS is the application when enabled can create alerts and pop-ups. To further test the XSS vulnerability please insert the following:
   <script>alert('vuln);</script> Hello!

To Exploit an SQL Injection Vulnerability in DVWA perform the following:

1. Exploit an SQL injection vulnerability by injecting SQL commands into the application's data entry fields and provide a screen shot or output of the attack
2. Power up the "TargetUbuntu01" Linux VM server and using your Instructor workstation's Internet Explorer, open a web browser as follows:
   http://172.30.0.x/dvwa, where x is IP host address that was DHCP'ed to the "TargetUbuntu01" Linux VM server
3. Once the web page comes up, login and click on the DVWA Security tab and set it to low. Then click on the SQL Injection tab which will provide us our vulnerable web app to test SQL injections against the back-end database.
4. We will try O'Malley as we want to see if the field populates any anomalies or errors. Did any character get recognized before our error?

5. We see from here that we can interrupt and possibly debug information from a different SQL injection. Let's try actually passing an SQL statement, try a' OR 'x'='x';#
6. Familiar statement to the infamous ***a' OR '1'&'1' #***
7. Several other combinations should also work, so let's try some.

NOTE: These strings are in clear text, you should check your Web Server logs specifically on Declare statements to know whether or not databases are being injected, and from these logs, check the databases for injected content. Obfuscation by using Hexadecimal character strings is also commonly used.

8. DB Enumeration a' ORDER BY 1;# not too different should show the login screen showing that it recognized the command, try 2 then 3 notice the difference between all 3 is 3 is not recognized as a value and the error relates to columns. Now we know we can start using Union Statements.
9. Try a' OR firstname IS NULL;# see error? Now try a' OR first_name IS NULL;# see the difference? The screen came back just like with our ORDER BY statement earlier.
10. Try a' OR database() LIKE 'DB';# This command searches for a possible hit on the DB's characters. Adding a % splits different fields to query. Try a' OR database() LIKE 'd%';# notice the output?
11. Try a' UNION SELECT table_schema, table_name FROM information_Schema.tables;# results in all Table and Column names as being used.
12. Try a' UNION ALL SELECT 1, @@version;# and that will give you some information on the version info for the SQL server.
13. Try a' UNION ALL SELECT system_user(),user();# this will tell you the user you are making queries under from the web app.
14. Try a' UNION ALL SELECT user, password FROM mysql.user;# priv;#' At this point you have a hash for a user to the backend DB.
15. We will check for injection at this time by issuing 'UNION SELECT 'test', '123' INTO OUTFILE 'testing1.txt. At this point we know we have a user, and we know the DB can be written to. We have users, user ID's, table and column information and an injectable database.

Deliverables

Upon completion of Lab #8: Perform a Website & Database Attack by Exploiting Identified Vulnerabilities, students are required to provide the following deliverables:

1. Lab #8 – Written Analysis of the Identified Vulnerabilities, Exploit, and Remediation Steps:
    a. A summary of findings, assessment, and recommendations report that includes:
        i. Enumeration – Identification of the Exploit
        ii. Compromise & Exploit
            1. Screenshot or description of the cross site scripting attack
            2. Screenshot or description of the SQL injection attack
        iii. Remediation
2. Lab #8 – Assessment Worksheet Questions & Answers

Evaluation Criteria and Rubrics

The following are the evaluation criteria and rubrics for Lab #8 that the students must perform:

1. Identify web application and web server backend database vulnerabilities as viable attack vectors – **[20%]**
2. Develop an attack plan to compromise and exploit a web site using cross-site scripting (XSS) against sample vulnerable web applications – **[20%]**
3. Conduct a manual Cross-site Scripting (XSS) attack against sample vulnerable web applications - **[20%]**
4. Perform SQL injection attacks against sample vulnerable web applications with e-commerce data entry fields – **[20%]**
5. Mitigate known web application and web server vulnerabilities with security countermeasures to eliminate risk from compromise and exploitation – **[20%]**

Lab #8 – Assignment Worksheet

Perform a Website & Database Attack by Exploiting Identified Vulnerabilities

Course Name & Number: ____

Student Name: ____

Instructor Name: ____

Lab Due Date: ____

Overview

Students must provide a Written Report of the Identified Vulnerabilities, Exploits, and Remediation Steps organized as follows:

Lab #8 – Assessment Worksheet

Perform a Website & Database Attack by Exploiting Identified Vulnerabilities

Course Name & Number: ______________________________

Student Name: ______________________________

Instructor Name: ______________________________

Lab Due Date: ______________________________

Overview

The students will verify and perform a Cross-site Scripting (XSS) exploit and an SQL Injection attack on the test bed web application and web server using the Damn Vulnerable Web App (DVWA) loaded on an Apache Web Server on "TargetUbuntu01" Linux VM server. They will first identify the IP target host, identify known vulnerabilities and exploits, and then attack the web application and web server using XSS and an SQL Injection to exploit the web application using a web browser and some simple command strings.

Lab Assessment Questions & Answers

1. Why is it critical to perform a penetration test on a web application prior to production implementation?
2. What is a cross-site scripting attack? Explain in your own words.
3. What is a reflective cross-site scripting attack?
4. What common method of obfuscation is used in most real world SQL attacks?
5. Which web application attack is more prone to extracting privacy data elements out of a database?
6. If you can monitor when SQL injections are performed on an SQL database, what would you recommend as a security countermeasure to monitor your production SQL databases?
7. Given that Apache and Internet Information Services (IIS) are the two most popular web application servers for Linux and Microsoft Windows platforms, what would you do to identify known software vulnerabilities and exploits?

8. What can you do to ensure that your organization incorporates penetrating testing and web application testing as part of its implementation procedures?

9. What other security countermeasures do you recommend for web sites and web application deployment to ensure the C-I-A of the web application?

10. Who is responsible and accountable for the C-I-A of production web applications and web servers?

Laboratory #9

Lab #9: Perform a Virus Scan and Malware Identification Scan and Eliminate Threats

Learning Objectives and Outcomes

Upon completing this lab, students will be able to complete the following tasks:

- Identify the risks associated with viruses, malware, and malicious software on a Windows Server
- Apply security countermeasures to mitigate the risk caused by viruses, malware, and malicious software
- Enable AVG as an anti-virus, malware, and malicious software security countermeasure on a Windows Server
- Disable unnecessary services in a Windows workstation and manually baseline enable processes
- Configure a Windows workstation internal firewall to block future malware infections from penetrating the system

Required Setup and Tools

This lab does not require the use of the ISS Mock IT Infrastructure - Cisco core backbone network. In addition, the Instructor VM workstation and Student VM workstations should be physically disconnected from the ITT internal network and be isolated on a dedicated layer 2 switch. This will allow for a shared DHCP server to be used to allocate the IP addresses for the instructor and student workstations. The following is required for this hands-on lab:

A) A classroom workstation (with at least 4 Gig RAM) capable of supporting an insert-able hard drive or USB hard drive with a pre-configured, virtualized server farm. This classroom workstation/server will support the virtualized server farm connected to the classroom layer 2 switch

B) An instructor workstation (with at least 2 Gig RAM) that shall act as the Instructor's demo LAB workstation. The instructor will display the Instructor workstation on the LCD projector to demo the loading and configuring of the ITT "Mock" IT Infrastructure and Server Farm with VMware Player

C) Students LAB workstations will use a local copy of the ITT "Mock" IT Infrastructure Server Farm on a local or USB hard drive with VMware Player to run their Student and Target VMs

The following summarizes the setup, configuration, and equipment needed to perform Lab #9:

1. A Virtualized Server Farm with:
   a. Microsoft DHCP server for allocating student IP host addresses
   b. A Student and/or Instructor VM workstation with Internet Explorer
2. Target VMs as described by the Lab:
   a. Windows 2003 Server Target VM 01
   b. AVG Antivirus and IZarc Archiver

   Windows 2003 Server Standard Edition

   - Windows Server 2003 Standard Edition 32-bit (VM Name: "TargetWindows01")
     - Computer Name: Windows02
     - Three Users Available: administrator, instructor or student (case sensitive)
     - Password: ISS316Security
     - IP Address: DHCP
     - Domain Login: NO
   - FTP (Filezilla FTP Server)
     - Port: 21
     - Username: instructor or student
     - Password: <blank>
   - TFTP (Tftpd32 TFTP Server)
     - Port: 69
     - Username: <none>
     - Password: <blank>
3. Standard ITT ISS onsite student workstation must have the following software applications loaded to perform this lab:
   a. VMware Player 3.x
   b. Microsoft Office 2007 or higher for Lab Assessment Questions & Answers

Recommended Procedures

Hands-on Lab #9: – Student Steps:

Students should perform the following steps:

1. Connect the student removable hard drive to your workstation
2. Power-up and log into your Student VM and "TargetWindows01" VM. Obtain an IP address from the DHCP Server on the classroom layer 2 switch

> Note: Remember if you only have 2 Gig RAM, you can power-on two VM's simultaneously to run this hands-on lab. "Student" VM and the "TargetWindows01" VM server.

3. Power up and login into the Instructor VM and "TargetWindows01" VM
   a. Login ID: "student" (case sensitive)
   b. Password: "ISS316Security" (case sensitive)
4. On the "TargetWindows01" VM, make sure the prodrev.zip file is on the desktop. This is an encrypted zip file with a password
5. Click on "AVG Free 9" icon on your desktop, and perform an update by clicking on update now, no internet access will be available but before scanning any file this should be the first step
6. Next click on Computer Scanner and for now pick the Scan Specific files or folders option and select the desktop to be scanned. Then click Start Scan option
7. This scan will return no infected files, given that encrypted files cannot be opened for scanning by Anti-virus software
8. Open the prodrev.zip file now using IZarc archiver by right clicking the file and clicking the extract here option. (See Screen 3)
9. Enter the files decryption password (password123), and you should now see a PDF file on the desktop named productreview.pdf.
10. Repeat Step 4 in AVG, and it should pick up a malicious virus found exploit by looking at the scan results for the most recent scan
11. Disable un-needed services in your Student VM workstation:
    a. Right click "My Computer" and click "Manage"
    b. Click on "Services" from the left side tree menu
    c. Select the desired service, open the context menu and select 'Properties'
    d. Change "Startup Type" to "Manual" or "Disable" then choose 'OK'

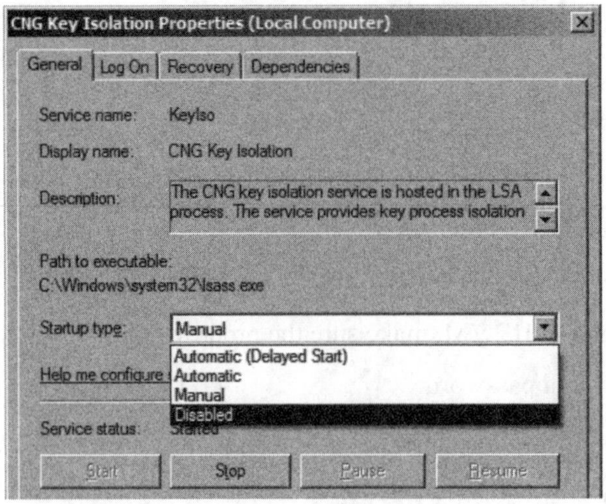

Figure 14 – Disable Windows Service

12. Document all services that are disabled.
13. Launch Windows Firewall: Start -> Administrative Tools -> Windows Firewall
14. Clicked "Advanced"
15. Identify the default ICMP settings for the internal Windows Server firewall in your Student VM workstation

Deliverables

Upon completion of this lab, students are required to provide the following deliverables:

1. Lab #9 – Students should provide a document, in Microsoft Word format, containing the following information:
   - A description of any identified un-needed services running on the Student VM workstation along with a description of the suggested action that should be taken to secure each service.
   - A description of at least three ICMP firewall rules that can be changed on the Student VM workstation to enhance C-I-A
   - A screenshot of their PDF submission to Virus Total of the malicious PDF
2. Lab #9 – Lab Assessment Questions & Answers

Evaluation Criteria and Rubrics

The following are the evaluation criteria and rubrics for Lab #9 that the students must perform:

1. Was the student able to identify the risks associated with viruses, malware, and malicious software on a Windows Server? – **[20%]**
2. Was the student able to apply security countermeasures to mitigate the risk caused by viruses, malware, and malicious software? – **[20%]**
3. Was the student able to enable AVG as an anti-virus, malware, and malicious software security countermeasure on a Windows Server? – **[20%]**
4. Was the student able to disable unnecessary services in a Windows workstation and manually baseline enable processes? – **[20%]**
5. Was the student able to configure a Windows workstation internal firewall to block future malware infections from penetrating the system? – **[20%]**

Lab #9 – Assessment Worksheet

Perform a Virus Scan and Malware Identification Scan and Eliminate Threats

Course Name & Number: ______________________________

Student Name: ______________________________

Instructor Name: ______________________________

LAB Due Date: ______________________________

Overview

In this lab the students learn how to use AVG Anti-virus for Windows to identify malware found on a compromised system. They will also examine the services enabled in their Windows workstation and disable unnecessary applications and processes. Finally, the students will examine the default configurations of a Windows workstation internal firewall.

LAB Assessment Questions & Answers

1. What is the main difference between a Trojan and a Virus?

2. A virus or malware can impact which of the three tenets of information systems security? C-I-A? Describe how it impacts it as well.

3. Once a file is found malicious on your computer, what are the default settings for USB/removable device scanning? What should an organization do regarding use of USB hard drives and slots on existing computers and devices?

4. Why is it recommended to do an anti-virus signature file update before performing an anti-virus scan on your computer?

5. When sending a file a user asks you to zip it and encrypt the file if possible, why would this be?

6. You receive an email regarding a link from one of your friends for some special documents, shortly after that you receive the same email from 3 other friends and the emails are not being blocked, what is likely the cause?

7. Specify a setting you would want to turn on if you were running AVG on your system to improve the quality of scans you do on the system?

8. Your employees e-mail file attachments to each other and externally through the organization's firewall and Internet connection. What security countermeasures can you implement to help mitigate the risk of rogue e-mail attachments and URL web links?

9. What are typical indicators that your computer system is compromised?

10. What elements are needed in a Workstation Domain policy regarding use of anti-virus and malicious software prevention tools?

Laboratory #10

Lab #10: Craft an Information Systems Security Policy

Learning Objectives and Outcomes

Upon completing this lab, students will be able to complete the following tasks:

- Define the policy definition for expected behavior by users, system administrators, management, and security personnel through the use of proper information security policy writing skills
- Define and authorize the consequences of violations to an information security policy by properly documenting them in said security policy
- Define the company consensus baseline stance on security regarding a specific issue or process and how it should be handled
- Minimize risk for the company by properly documenting and proactively addressing potential security needs or scenarios
- Track compliance with regulations and legislation by providing a framework for best practice that can be followed by all employees

Required Setup and Tools

This is a paper-based, hands-on LAB and does not require the use of the ISS "Mock" IT infrastructure or Virtualized Server Farm.

The following summarizes the setup, configuration, and equipment needed to perform Lab #1:

1. Standard ITT ISS onsite student workstation must have the following software applications loaded to perform this lab:
    a. Microsoft Office 2007 or higher for Assessment Worksheet Questions & Answers and reviewing and drafting the Information Security Policy Templates made available by SANS.org: http://www.sans.org/security-resources/policies/

Recommended Procedures

Hands-on Lab #10 – Student Steps:

Students should perform the following steps:

1. Research the importance of Information Security Policy writing and how Policies differ from Processes and Guidelines.
2. Research some of the most commonly use Information Security Policies and, if possible, review whatever existing policies are in place for ITT-Tech.

3. Browse to SANS.org at the following link and open for review the document with a recommended Security Policy Roadmap - Process for Creating Security Policies: http://www.sans.org/reading_room/whitepapers/policyissues/security-policy-roadmap-process-creating-security-policies_494
4. Review the main sections of Section 4 Information Gathering:
   a. Identify Assets
   b. Identify Vulnerabilities and Threats
   c. Evaluation of Measures and Controls
5. Review the main sections in Section 7 Writing Policy:
   a. Securing Hardware, Peripherals And Other Equipment
   b. Controlling Access To Information And Systems
   c. Purchasing And Maintaining Commercial Software
   d. Developing And Maintaining In-House Software
   e. Combating Cyber Crime
   f. Complying With Legal And Policy Requirements
   g. Planning For Business Continuity
   h. Addressing Personnel Issues Relating To Security
   i. Controlling E-Commerce Information Security
   j. Delivering Training And Staff Awareness
   k. Dealing With Premises Related Considerations
   l. Detecting And Responding To IS Incidents
   m. Classifying Information And Data
6. Browse to SANS.org at the following link and open for review the document with a recommended Information Security Policy Development Guide for Large and Small Companies: http://www.sans.org/reading_room/whitepapers/policyissues/information-security-policy-development-guide-large-small-companies_1331
7. Review the main sections in Section 8 Policy Development Lifecycle
   a. Senior Management Buy-in
   b. Determine a Compliance Grace Period
   c. Determine Resource Involvement
   d. Review Existing Policy
   e. Determine Research Materials
   f. Interview SMEs

g. Write Initial Draft
h. Style Considerations
i. Review Cycles
j. Review with Additional Stakeholders
k. Policy Gap Identification Process
l. Develop Communication Strategy
m. Publish
n. Activate Communication Strategy
o. Regularly Review and Update

8. Review the main sections in Section 9 Policy Document Outline
    a. Introduction
    b. Purpose
    c. Scope
    d. Roles and Responsibilities
    e. Sanctions and Violations
    f. Revisions and Updating Schedule
    g. Contact information
    h. Definitions/Glossary
    i. Acronyms
9. Navigate with your browser to the SANS Security Policy Project web page http://www.sans.org/security-resources/policies/, scroll to the bottom of the page and review the available templates for Information Security Policies. Pick out an information security policy template and fill it out based on the fictitious company discussed in Lab #6: Business Continuity Planning.

Deliverables

Students are required to provide the following deliverables as part of the Lab #10 – Craft an Information Systems Security Policy:

1. Lab #10 – Written Information System Security Policy based on one of the templates provided by the SANS Institute made for the fictitious company introduced in Lab #6 Business Continuity Planning
2. Lab #10 – Lab Assessment Questions & Answers

Evaluation Criteria and Rubrics

The following are the evaluation criteria and rubrics for Lab #10 that the students must perform:

1. Was the student able to define the policy definition for expected behavior by users, system administrators, management, and security personnel through the use of proper information security policy writing skills? – **[50%]**
2. Was the student able to define and authorize the consequences of violations to an information security policy by properly documenting them in said security policy? – [1**0%**]
3. Was the student able to define the company consensus baseline stance on security regarding a specific issue or process and how it should be handled? – **[10%]**
4. Was the student able to mitigate risk for the company by properly documenting and proactively addressing potential security needs or scenarios? – **[20%]**
5. Was the student able to track compliance with regulations and legislation by providing a framework for best practice that can be followed by all employees? – **[10%]**

Lab #10 – Assessment Worksheet

Craft an Information Systems Security Policy

Course Name & Number: ______________________________

Student Name: ______________________________

Instructor Name: ______________________________

LAB Due Date: ______________________________

Overview

The students will research the benefits of writing and maintaining Information Security Policies which help to ensure that risk is minimized and that any security incidents are effectively responded to. Information security policy defines the organization's attitude to information, and announces internally and externally that information is an asset, the property of the organization, and it is to be protected from unauthorized access, modification, disclosure, and destruction. The instructor will also guide the students through the Security Policy Roadmap and Development Guides provided by the SANS Institute and determine what type of information security policy they will be writing for their fictitious organization.

Lab Assessment Questions & Answers

1. What is a Policy? Give an example of an information systems security policy.
2. What is a Standard? Give an example of an information systems security standard.
3. What is a Guideline?
4. Name 5 different sample policy templates available by SANS Institute.
5. Give an example of a sanction or violation that can be imposed on an employee that performs a breach of an information security policy.
6. Submit your written policy using one of the policy templates you downloaded from the SANS Institute website.